A GUIDE TO THE NEW ECONOMIC CITIZENSHIP

EASING ECON-ANGST

E. ROBERT ERBE

ISBN: E-Book # 978-1-962132-55-8

Paperback # 978-1-962132-56-5

Hardback # 978-1-962132-57-2

Printed in United States of America

Library of Congress Reg. # 2023919635

Cover Design by: Amazon Publishing Inc, NYC, New York, USA

Publisher: Amazon Publishing Inc, NYC, New York, USA

For permission requests, please contact: info@amazonpublishinginc.co

CONTENTS

DEDICATION

This work is dedicated to the many students who have challenged me to understand them and see economics through their eyes and minds.

INTRODUCTION

In my first undergraduate economics course, my professor began the class by saying, *"I have a three-step foolproof way to make a million dollars,"* and that he would tell us at the end of class. He suspected that most of the class was taking Economics with the hope of becoming wealthy. It was a great hook. The entire class listened attentively and took notes for the forty-minute lecture. At the end of class, he said, "*the first step was to get a million dollars.*" It was my first lesson in economics: using incentives to motivate people.

Since that first class, I embarked on a study of how the American economy worked, and how a myriad of actors could be organized to prosper. I found early on that the answer lay in the dynamics of self-interest operating in a competitive market system, that using incentives as rewards provided for society's wants and needs. I saw how millions of Americans were incentivized to work hard by following self-interests.[1]

Americans in the later decades of the 20th Century became accustomed to working additional part-time jobs or having two full-time jobs within a family to maintain their standard of living. Today, the average American adult works 38.7 hours, and Americans aged 25-54 work an average of 40.2 hours per week.[2] Americans work more hours than their European counterparts[3].

Since its beginning, the American economy had two characteristics that played an important role in its development. They were economic freedom and competitive opportunities. For centuries, immigrants flocked to the United States to taste the freedoms of choosing and profiting from opportunities. They wanted a better life for themselves and their children. Citizens seized upon various educational paths, work environments, and locales in a country without internal borders. They were motivated by self-interest.

As the United States' economy grew and became more complex, groups of actors accumulated economic power in the economy's sectors; however, many Americans found their economic freedom decreasing and opportunities becoming dim. Ceilings and restrictions were placed on minorities and gender. Social mobility and economic advancement felt slower. Lower-income classes became mired in situational and generational traps. Economic advice was provided that was free or subscribed to. It was readily available and possibly helpful. But it did not speak to the reality of many families.

Today, citizens in the American economy live under this umbrella of economic freedom, competing for a higher standard of living. However, with economic success, there has developed an emotional and logical disconnect. Is everyone really happy? The song says, *"Don't worry, be happy."* Maybe.

The disconnect occurs between consumers' desire to shop until they drop and economists' message to conserve scarce resources. Expectations of happiness through material abundance are raised through the media's marketing of the "good life." But economists view the "good life" differently. They raise the existential specter of the planet's scarcity. *Consumer Abundance vs. Resource Scarcity is on the fight card for the 21st Century.*

Modern media messaging provides mounds of information about employment, financial literacy, businesses, consumption, and sales. "Buy this, move here, pay later, invest now, don't miss the opportunity." But there is something missing in the overwhelming and confusing economic news and messaging. There is a sea of information *about* the economy, markets, stocks and bonds, businesses, financial literacy, work and careers, and national economic statistics. But what do we do with it?

Unanswered questions have become the public's new economic reality.

- *What must I know to understand the new economic forces that are defining the economy and my place on its ladder?*
- *How do I create a vantage point for navigating the changes?*
- *I can see the economy out the window, but can I see where I fit?*
- *Where is my economic portrait?*
- *I am motivated, but why am I so anxious about deciding which path to take for success?*
- *Do I have the directional know-how?*

It is as if we are in a space capsule surrounded by powerfully complex technologies to take us on wonderful trips. There are signs and information describing the technology that is keeping us alive. The problem is we don't have the skills or knowledge to *operate* the technology. Are we doomed?

The 20th Century's technology has exploded in all sectors of economic life, from production to purchase. Consumers must have new skills of password-protocol digitalization for purchasing goods and services through television QR codes, internet sites, smart phones, and enrollments in purchase-cycling programs and clubs. Almost all career and job categories require digital and computer skills. Jobs are giving way to the installation of technology, automation, and robotics. Artificial Intelligence is threatening many jobs and careers. At the same time, the planet's systems of biogeochemical cycles, ecologies, and climate are being existentially threatened by human population crowding and economic activities.

Corporate power, technological progress, and environmental perversion have changed the economic atmosphere in which we live. Change is the dynamic propelling us into the future. At the same time, people's time references are spread across the late 20th Century and the first decades of the 21st Century. The population consists of those with various mixtures of analog and digital skills and cultures.

The public's well-being would benefit from a well-marked guide to the new century's economic citizenship.

The positive results of economic freedom have been 230 years in the making, but our road to success feels crowded and not well-marked. This led to the second part of the answer of how the economy works, and it resides within the emotions and psyche of American workers and owners. It is the underside of freedom. Those traveling the road to success possess an underlying insecurity and unease about their place, knowledge, and status in the economy. Economic freedom is packaged with economic stress. It is an uncomfortable responsibility. *I might know about the economy, but I am stressed about how to live in it.*

Economic education can provide the economic knowledge to generate steadiness in addressing decisions. However, an individual who is unprepared carries a heightened unpleasant feeling of economic peril.

Anxiety surfaces when facing life's questions in a complex competitive economy. Self-doubting questions arise, "Am I going to make it?" "Is this the right time?," or "Am I going to lose out?." They appear in many contexts and ways. *The presence of this anxiety is the cost of economic freedom.* It is the emotional baggage carried on the way to economic well-being. Playing the *real* economic game without understanding the rules, moves, and strategies can make a player nervous, unsettled, frustrated, or aggravated.

There is a treasure of economic knowledge found in the social science of economics. The view of the economy and economic concepts provides support and preparation for economic citizenship. However, the public knows very little about the social science of economics, and what is known is probably wrong, for example:

1. Demand is a quantity.
2. Supply is a quantity.

3. The stock markets are good measures of the economy.
4. Everyone has a good chance to become wealthy.
5. Wealth is money.
6. Money is backed by gold.
7. Gold is wealth.
8. America is the healthiest country in the world.
9. America is the freest country in the world.
10. Americans are the richest citizens in the world.
11. Technological innovation is the answer to environmental degradation.
12. More is better than less.

There are economic theories and facts that show that each of the above is incorrect (see Appendix). What we need are correct economic concepts that empower us by adding value to our lives and defining a new economic citizenship. They will ease anxiety and improve well-being.

Economics has the mission of improving well-being and enriching citizens' lives through economic growth. Economic growth is a top goal of America's economy, but it can mask the problems of individuals' well-being. Well-being is embodied in the mastery of economic citizenship where citizens understand and practice their economic rights and responsibilities. It places citizens in the larger economy, not just in a daily workstation or ownership chair. It is being able to see the larger maze, not just to take the road's fork of right or left. Economics' mission is to prepare and educate in order to fulfill the promise of well-being and participate in growing the economy.

Unfortunately, preparing for economic citizenship has been neglected. There is an economic knowledge deficit in America. The lessons in economic education have been, to a large extent, forfeited to the hours of commercials and digital advertising that children and adults absorb. Their lesson is "*happiness = buying stuff.*" And it may be buying stuff that we didn't know we needed. This commercialism produces highly motivated and knowledgeable consumers but also establishes a kind of anxiety. *Can I afford happiness? Can I anticipate and overcome economic competition, dangers, and problems? Is there a job or career in the economy that can support a comfortable lifestyle?*

In 2023, there were about 170M workers in the American labor force. Workers endured economic anxiety about taking their place in the labor force because of a deficit in economic education. Anxiety was their companion along the way. Economic success was mastered by some who wrested the path to a high standard of living. Others used it to construct a middle-class life, while others found the misfortune of languishing in poverty. In each case, citizens have had to deal with continual emotional stress.

A portion of the employee experience is the constant concerns for job security and career viability. A portion of the business owner's experience is the constant concerns of consumer acquisition, supply chains, labor quality, and profit margin. The economy's complexity and volatility signal warnings. Employees harbor a baseline of worries, feeling that they may not be flexible, skilled, or knowledgeable enough to successfully navigate the future. Small business owners work tirelessly to stay ahead of the competition and the costs of doing business. Who has time to understand the system's economic citizenship?

Economic citizenship begins with achieving satisfying jobs, careers, or business ownership, and ends with being a smart consumer. It is complicated by the public's current and insufficient state of economic knowledge. A lifeful of decisions lacks effective economic guidance. Living with knowledge shortfalls produces undue anxiety. Even after decisions are made, employees and business owners continue to endure feelings of insecurity and unease. This increased economic anxiety of the 21st Century is here called *Econ-Angst*, and our mission is to mitigate it by following markers of economic principles.

Finally, I came to redefine economic citizenship. There seems to be a seismic shift in the economic landscape. It has to do with reviewing the anxiety levels of economic changes. The new century demands a new view of economic citizenship. Econ-Angst has increased because self-interest, economic freedom, economic competition, economic growth, and profit-seeking have been altered. There are impending dangers to social coherence and environmental health. A new economic citizenship must lower Econ-Angst to improve public's health, outlook, and well-being. Self-interest must be tempered by social and environmental interests. Economic growth must be re-evaluated for resource scarcity. Economic freedom must be constrained to properly manage the planet's resources. Profit-seeking and economic competition must be relegated to *one of many goals* of economic activity.

Principles of the social science of economics are discussed here, but this is not an economics textbook. Textbooks present the structure of economic theory, spending chapters on the various topics, details, and examples of how economists study the economy. A standard textbook will describe economics and its economic principles as a formidable theoretical castle from afar. We will become familiar with most of these principles; however, *we will change our perspective by explaining how individuals use these principles. It is an applied use of economic principles to educate for the new economic citizenship and decrease Econ-Angst.* The following chapters will identify ten markers of key economic principles. They are called *Economic Cairns.*

Applying economic principles will not guarantee success, but they will make you a better economic citizen and ease the path to success.

Remember, I still hold that three-step way to make a million dollars. OK. But I also have a ten-step solution for economic anxiety.

The first step is to just relax and keep reading.

CHAPTER 1

HIGHLIGHTS

ECON-ANGST

- *Economic education does not prepare citizens to live in the American economy.*
- *The sources of economic stress cannot be eliminated.*
- *Media messaging interferes with citizens' ability to make correct economic decisions.*
- *A gaming approach to the economy adds to economic stress.*
- *Media messaging is not similarly received by diverse citizens.*

- *Without understanding economic concepts and consequences, citizens facing economic decisions feel trepidation that breeds fear and anxiety.*
- *Econ-Angst is the pervasive and general feeling of unease and anxiety caused by economic stressors.*
- *Using key economic concepts eases Econ-Angst on the path to success.*

ECONOMIC CITIZENSHIP

- *Economic citizenship begins with the roles and responsibilities that citizens have in the economy.*
- *Economic citizenship nurtures self-reliance and understanding of its rights and responsibilities.*
- *Economic citizenship realizes the challenges of economic freedom and the diversity of citizens' values.*

- *Economic citizenship faces the economic imperative to attain and manage a desirable standard of living.*

LIFE IN AMERICA

"Anxiety is the dizziness of freedom."

--Soren Kierkegaard.

"Despair is a narcotic. It lulls the mind into indifference."

--Charlie Chaplin.

ECON-ANGST

Is there an educational hole in preparation for economic citizenship? You bet. Many American students did not take economics as a social science in high school. High school economics across the land appear as courses in Practical Economics, Business and Personal Finance, or economic topics within United States or world history. Economic literacy is narrowly centered around financial topics. The 2022 Council for Economic Education's Survey of the States found that only twenty-five states required a course in economic education, and twenty-three were courses in personal finance.[1] This is a practical topic under the umbrella of economics; however, the social science of economics if it appears at all, is relegated only to some college preparation tracks. Economic concepts necessary for citizenship are a forgotten or missing component of the crowded high school curriculum. A Council for Economic Education (2020) study concluded that ". . . economic issues remain almost entirely absent from the broader K–12 social studies curriculum, resulting in a failure to engage young people in some of the most pressing moral and civic issues of our times."[2]

What about higher education? Many college majors do not have a social science economics choice or requirement. This omission at the collegiate level contributes to economic insecurity and anxiety. In The Ohio State University's Office of Student Life 2020 study, economic insecurity was found in 74% of respondents who were stressed about their personal finances in general.[3] Over 33% of college students nationwide felt that their academic progress was negatively impacted by financial issues with stress being the constant feeling of anxiety.[4]

Economic anxiety that begins in America's college-age students is present as a general feeling of unease and anxiety caused by economic stressors. Econ-Angst is physically and emotionally damaging to citizens. Econ-Angst changes behaviors and attitudes that can be harmful to health and interfere with bodily functions.

Surveys, indexing, and articles have explored this harm caused by economic anxiety. WebMD has identified the mental health issue of "scarcity mentality".[5] Associated with economic insecurity, it is described as an obsession with something that you can't get, a mindset of the brain's background noise, which occurs as a feeling of deprivation or longing—usually for time or money. It lowers IQ and limits brain function. It is heightened during economic downturns. Coming out of the COVID-19 pandemic, COVID anxiety's top place was replaced by economic anxiety[6].

Economic stressors are pervasive. In 2015, Verywell Mind's Economic Anxiety Index found anxiety widespread in America,[7] with about 50% in the index sample anxious about the economy, 25% having lost sleep, and 66% sometimes or frequently anxious about their financial situation. The 2017 American Psychological Association (APA) *State of Our Nation* reported that over 60% of Americans surveyed found work and money to be a source of stress[8]. The 2019 APA *Stress in America Survey* reported that 64% of adults reported money and work as top stressors; and, among Gen Zs, personal debt (33%) and housing instability (31%) were significant sources of stress, while 28 percent additionally cited food availability[9]. The 2020 Marketplace-Edison Research Poll reported that 35% of respondents lost sleep over personal economic concerns[10]. The 2022 APA's Stress in American Survey noted that the majority of adults said the economy (69%) and money (66%) were significant sources of stress.[11]

On life's economic journey, the systemic sources of stress cannot be eliminated; however, stress can be eased by understanding and using Economic Cairns. Unfortunately, these markers have been omitted, misplaced, or lost along the way.

Educational learning routines have added to the stress. School graduates have followed the standard educational routine: first, learn the lesson, then, take the test. But this is not helpful when following life's routine. Life reverses it. Citizens are continually tested by life, then learn their lesson! Learning by making mistakes can be useful in class, but, in life's economic journey where important decisions are made, this reversal of routine is costly, emotionally demanding, and full of Econ-Angst. This angst takes its toll on citizens and interferes with achieving success.

Economic freedom, a cornerstone of American economic citizenship, requires smart decision-making from childhood to later life. It would be difficult to imagine a life without it. This freedom provides economic rights that can be used for success. But in a fast-paced and changing economy, jumping into a traditional job or the easiest career may not be the right choice. Economic freedom may present an array of opportunities. However, citizens may not be fully informed about the economic consequences or may not consider the economic future. Citizens do their best to choose a path for their economic life; but, far too many times, it becomes a Do-It-Yourself journey to a job that is a moving target. It is *not* fully understood that, with this freedom, comes the *necessity to navigate* the stressors and insecurity. Without understanding basic economic concepts and consequences, citizens may feel trepidation in facing life's economic decisions. Over time, trepidation breeds fear and Econ-Angst at life's junctures.

There is baseline uneasiness in the lives of families and the workforce. Worry becomes part of the day, especially when there is an incomplete social safety net, social prejudices, disappearing civil rights, or economic storm clouds. There are citizens who start at third base, but most pay to get into the batter's box. American business and employment fields are not level. Latinxs and African Americans face a different playing field than white Americans. Women face a different playing field that men.

Americans harbor increased Econ-Angst when addressing issues such as financial debt, job and occupation choices, health care, government regulations, or unemployment. The 21st Century has added issues concerning the effects of Artificial Intelligence, digital tech advances, globalization, and robotic automation. Econ-Angst also has the effect of skewing career and job selection. The popular career website, *Handshake* (2023)[12], reported that Gen Z's searches and applications showed a priority for job stability. Those of employment age moved away from large-salary corporate and technology jobs and toward those in government, law, and politics. The report also noted that this age range matured during the lingering stressors of the Great Recession (2007-09) and the COVID-19 pandemic (2020-23).

The hours and days of worry given to economic responsibility become the emotional price paid for economic freedom. The price varies across population income levels. A higher price is borne by lower socio-economic groups that lack sufficient personal resources to address economic stressors.

There are also *dollar costs* for loss of work time due to stress-related illnesses and conditions, both for the individual and for society. Econ-Angst increases medical costs. *Healthline* reported that stress results in "accidents, absenteeism, employee turnover, diminished productivity, and direct medical, legal, and insurance costs" that cost the United States $300 billion every year.[13]

Econ-Angst arises while framing many of life's questions.

- *How can I balance short and long-term debt?*

- *What training or education is needed for the digital economy?*
- *Should the firm invest in more automation and technology and shrink employee numbers?*
- *What job or occupation is best to prepare for my age?*
- *How can my generational poverty be averted or overcome?*
- *What occupation is going to attain and maintain a family's middle-class quality of life?*
- *How can I keep wealth secure and increasing?*
- *What knowledge base and skill set are needed to face the demands of automation, technology, and Artificial Intelligence?*

Using key economic concepts mitigates the personal and social costs incurred by the worry and anxiety that are associated with making decisions, finding resolutions, and discovering answers. However, using economic concepts seems so far from the demands of daily living, even though they could smooth the path toward success and well-being. What is the alternative?

Economic concepts can mollify the stress of economic citizenship, but lacking economic concepts, citizens sometimes turn to negative alternatives for relief. These strategies embody gamblers' hopes of the one-time magic bullet even when missing the shot leaves Econ-Angst stronger than before. Wrong answers or no solutions remain, with the probability of success slimmer and slimmer. For many of the economy's participants and stakeholders, the current path to economic investment and income success resembles winning in a game of chance—all or nothing. Dreaming of sudden increases in asset markets, prizes, coupons, and club points comes easily. However, a big payoff of a lucky play in a casino game or lottery is improbable and results in few winners and many losers. Anticipating winning helps satisfy the need for quick answers to problems and issues. One can become a winner through chance and luck (Is there really such a thing?) of the game or by accumulating enough purchase points. One can "win" by clicking the right coupon or scratching the right card. This participation is full of fleeting excitement and temporary release of anxiety, but the odds are against citizens. They are slanted toward benefiting those running the games, helping government budgets and business profits. The least able to lose are the most likely to gamble. This gaming environment hides or eliminates responsible economic behavior. Econ-Angst deepens in this *fantasy economy* driven by the material culture of consumerism[14].

Not all Americans have the same starting line, running lane, possess the same tools, or have the same expectations. Americans are not a homogenized group. There is the constant clash of "us vs. them" prejudices-Black/White, Jew/Antisemite, Brown/White, Immigrant/White Nationalist, Young/Elderly, Middle America/Coastal America, North/South, Female/Male, Urban/Country, Rich/Poor, Straight/LGBTQ+, and Democrat/Republican/Independent. Enough? Are there more?

Social and economic tensions remain as complications to economic citizenship; however, by overcoming these prejudices, one can take steps toward reducing tension. *Economic and social prejudices are harmful to economic efficiency, economic growth, and social cohesion.* What happens when one group advances faster than another? Does it result in attitudes of jealousy, calls of unfairness, or deepening divisiveness?

Economic advancement is a cause for celebration. The economy is *not a zero-sum game* where a positive move is canceled by a negative response. There exists competition for economic roles; no one should own them. But the new economic citizenship recognizes that improvement for one is not at the *cost* of another. A dynamic economy opens additional opportunities for those who are prepared. In June 2023, the Bureau of Labor Statistics reported almost 10 million *unfilled jobs* in the economy.

Social mobility spurs growth that improves opportunities. Social diversity is a strength that enriches the American economy. All able citizens need to be value-added workers reaching their potential. When this happens, the economy's productive output increases. More and higher valued-added wages increase consumer spending, driving economic growth and full employment. Larger employment lanes and fair hiring practices heal intergroup bias. However, existing socially divisive attitudes and discrimination show up as costs that weaken the economy and increase bias. A CITI Group study found that, between 2000 and 2020, the U.S. economy lost $16 trillion in Gross Domestic Product due to discrimination against African Americans[15]. A paper by the World Economic Forum found that racial and ethnic discrimination cost the U.S. economy $52 trillion between 1990 and 2021[16]. National economic losses increase insecurity and spread Econ-Angst in the population.

Socially divisive attitudes and discrimination occur within the American media's $300+ billion advertising and marketing machine. American media focuses on profit. Advertising plays a large part. Groups' differences of gender, ethnicity, race, age, and regional locations show up in cultural characteristics of vocabulary, foods, dress, music, ideas, truths, goals for the future, and biases. Advertising appeals are designed toward herd mentality, sexuality, or self-concept issues. Advertising applies these characteristics to increase sales of products or use of services. Ads also ask for votes, or to support special interests, or join consumer clubs for discounts. The flood of advertising spots and pop-ups celebrates consumption as society's dominant and ideal way of life. The messages play to individual self-interest but, in doing so, can solidify and aggravate society's differences. Advertising targets age or cultural groups. People are portrayed as gender or socially stereotypical images adding to us/them bias.

Modern communications present an advertising tidal wave to consumers. Unlimited shopping and buying opportunities are at the internet's fingertip, the TV or radio, or the QR Code. You don't have to get up from the couch. Purchases show up at the door. Make a phone call or click the website to use the drive-thru or pick-up window. Yes,

America's citizens are immersed in the global media buzz of unending advertising voices and images that are available without leaving their rooms, cars or even moving at all

- *In 2022, there were 15,000 active radio stations*[17] *and 1,758 broadcast television networks*[18] *in the United States that maneuvered for eye and ear time.*
- *In 2023, U.S. advertising was estimated to be $352 billion.*[19]
- *Americans show addictive behaviors to phone usage*[20]*.*
- *Flurry reports that Americans spend an average of 5 hours per day on their phones.*[21]

Advertising messages come visually, aurally, directly, subliminally, or via social media sites, and are packaged within entertaining and appealing sound and sight bites. Economic notions are absorbed as opinions and preferences from the media industry and culture that invade and occupy our public *and private* moments. The advertising industry has created unintended consequences of augmenting society's confusion and division. By targeting self-interest for profitability, the industry uses techniques that tug at biases, prejudices, me-only-attitudes, and self-absorption. Understandably, the industry's purpose is not to improve society's cohesion and civic health. But whose best interest is being sold? Is there a what's-best-for-me option? Am I alone in the economy? Are the messages promoting my best economic interest, my neighbors' best interest, my community's best interest, and the public's best interest all the same? Difficult to tell. This is a confusing and conflicting way to live as a responsible economic citizen. It feeds Econ-Angst.

What can be made of the dissonance and anxiety created by these endless messages? Can we control our happiness and purpose? Is it possible to live an intelligent economic life? Is everyone just a consumer who uses advertisers' choices to satisfy needs and unlimited wants? Economics opens a larger window beyond a consumer's life of choices. The new economic citizenship is an expanded life that includes responsibilities in the personal, social, and environmental spheres. A holistic economic life can be experienced. A better idea emerges. Distinguish whose self-interest is being promoted through advertising and at what cost. Examine your options and avenues to well-being. Everything must not boil down to personal consumption. It takes a more social perspective of cooperation and trust. Trust in the public sphere brings joy to the value of others and other groups. The economy depends upon businesses' and workers' cooperation to develop the trust necessary for the public good. Contracts can form a pathway of trust. Neighborhood groups and some social media sites can form a pathway of trust. Politicians and government officials, instead of suspicion, must form a pathway of trust. The success of a democratic economy depends on such pathways to diminish Econ-Angst. Well-being and trust are valuable feelings within a nation, but, unfortunately, have been diminishing. The economist, Arthur Okun's, Misery Index (see Appendix) tracks the sense of ill-being in the economy. It has been relatively high in the years 2021-23. The 2019 Pew Research Center's *Trust and Distrust in America* survey found about half of Americans surveyed had diminished trust in politics and government's ability to solve society's problems.

Economics opens conversations, not debates. Are we on the right or wrong track? This question is a good prompt to build cooperation and trust. Economic conversations among and between society's groups open a pathway to address decisions and lower Econ-Angst. Below are common anxiety-producing decisions *worthy of an economic conversation*:

- *to save or invest.*
- *to stay in school, get a job, or somehow do both,*
- *to buy now or buy later,*
- *to rent or buy,*
- *to play by the rules or bend the rules,*
- *to work hard or work smart,*
- *to be an employee, own your own business, or be your brand,*
- *to move or stay,*

- *to play it safe or take the risk,*
- *to gamble or abstain,*
- *to think it's only money or squeeze the dollar,*
- *to be selfish and greedy or make a village, and*
- *to trust in the system or beat the system.*

Citizens are exposed to conflicting and disturbing economic messages regarding consumer purchasing (more is better & retail therapy?), meaningful work (the grind of the rat race?), social responsibilities (look out for number one?), gambling (addiction?) and harmonious living (civic violence and high-walled media bubbles?). Society's messages come from institutions such as education, religion, news media, and government. They come from entertainment, social support groups, marketing and advertising, private sector companies, and family traditions. They muddle the individual's search for economic guidance.

Another source of confusion relates to how citizens filter messages. They are not interpreted the same way. Americans have different tastes, preferences, values, and opinions. They have constructed diverse perspectives that increase anxiety, confusion, and disheartening notions.

- *Is there a rank order of ideas?*
- *Are some messages worth more than others?*
- *Who should we listen to?*
- *Do I identify with the ideas of this group or that?*
- *Am I in a bubble of like minds?*
- *Can I even trust myself to choose wisely given the vast number of "economic experts"?*
- *Why am I paid less than someone else?*
- *What is economic citizenship anyway?*
- *Is it possible to pull back from the confusion to see a better perspective?*

The response to these questions begins with four thoughts:

1. Realizing the challenges and responsibilities of economic freedom,
2. Understanding the economy's cultural and demographic diversity,
3. Recognizing the universal economic imperative to gain and manage a desirable standard of living, and then
4. Embarking on a chosen journey using key economic concepts.

Understanding key economic concepts is not a formula for success, but a map to ease Econ-Angst on the journey.

ECONOMIC CITIZENSHIP

The concept of citizenship was created through war, force, treaty, and identity-building within societies. Citizenship became a political and national distinction. Laws and prejudicial power identified levels and types. Economic factors sharpened and defined full citizenship by the power of property and resource ownership. Worker status was defined by gender, ethnic group, race, slavery, and immigration. These factors distributed economic success and power unequally. Capitalism's freedom also created the importance of ability and intelligence differences as contributors to unequal economic outcomes. Citizens' economic status, along with natural differences in ability, are baked into the outcomes' dispersal of the American economy. They complicate the view of the economy. Some will see income and wealth outcomes as natural to the system. Others will see them as a flaw of the system. That conversation is worthy of exploration; however, it is outside of our purpose.

For our purpose, we will refer to economic citizenship as citizens' place and participation in the economy. It identifies economic rights and responsibilities that are the basis of earning a living and contributing to the common good. Economic citizenship is the sum of the roles and legal activities that citizens assume within the economy. These roles are defined by functions and pursuits such as a consumer, worker, producer, manager, seller, inventor, investor, or creator. Most citizens have more than one role. The roles' rights and responsibilities are informally and traditionally followed by citizens and maintained and enforced by governmental laws and organizational guidelines. The rights and responsibilities appear in community volunteer memberships, office rules, union rules, business contract stipulations, consumer rights, tax laws, business and corporate regulations, and a vast array of legal rights, remedies, and actions.

Economic citizenship is nurtured by the values of self-reliance, personal and social responsibility. Adam Smith referred to the moral character of what is honorable and noble about citizens in social life. This citizenship requires *adhering to responsibilities of the public good.* Americans' economic rights start with freedom of self-determination and a combined sense of independence and interdependence. Citizens' actions occur within the legal structure and protection of the Constitution and laws of the United States.

Immigration made America what Eleanor Roosevelt called a "nation of nations." Waves of non-slave immigrants dating from the colonial period to today have followed their idea of the "American Dream" to take advantage of political, religious, social, and economic freedoms.[21] Economic citizenship has harbored motivation to improve socio-economic life through accomplishment, talent, and merit of work. The dream of the gold-paved road, however, was found to have many bumps and potholes. New citizens had to overcome tax burdens, regulations, social prejudices, false prophets, and competition, as well as the chutes and ladders of the economy's busts and booms.

Economic rights that cover institutional protection, fairness, and bias have been disputed. America's freedom of speech and democratic principles have been exercised in historical arguments about such economic-political issues as

- *citizenship's definition,*
- *voting rights,*

- *affirmative action,*
- *labor rights to organize and strike,*
- *the power of monopolies, oligopolies, trusts and holding companies,*
- *copyrights and patents,*
- *taxation and regulation,*
- *corporate collusion and cooperation,*
- *right-to-work laws,*
- *public health as a civil right,*
- *immigrants' citizenship status,*
- *racial, gender, age, and LGBTQ+ civil and work-place rights,*
- *educational rights, and*
- *inequity issues of the economic system.*

Citizens have the responsibility to enter a job, occupation, or position that contributes to their well-being, but the responsibility must be more than that. The 21st Century has changed the nature of America's economy. There are factors that go beyond the characteristics of last century's economy. A new economic citizenship must meet the challenges. *The new economic citizenship must expand to include responsibilities to society and stewardship of the earth.*

The new economic citizenship's responsibility has developed *new elements*:

- *The responsibility to compete and work for self-interest must include to work for the public good,*
- *The freedom to advance individual economic opportunity must include to further advance opportunities for all segments of the population,*
- *The rights of property ownership and contract must include the existential right and usage of earth's resources.*

The newly responsible economic citizen finds well-being and satisfaction in roles that are valuable to self, society, and the planet. The fully enhanced responsibility is to contribute to oneself and family, to contribute to social cohesion, and to contribute to the planet's health. Corporate and business economic citizenship must include proper stewardship of the environment in productive activities, contribution to the public sphere, and care for employee well-being.

At the heart of the American economy resides the responsibility of workers to find a job or career where public good, work's value, sufficient wage, and promotion of the earth's sustainability intersect.

At the heart of the American economy resides the responsibility of the business community to efficiently produce goods and services where protection of the environment, public good, and care for workers' lives intersect.

At the heart of economic freedom resides decisions that discover, create, and practice individual, public, business, environmental, and social well-being.

CHAPTER 2

HIGHLIGHTS

ECONOMICS: A SOCIAL SCIENCE

- *The social science of economics gets confused with economists' occupations and where they are employed.*
- *Economics is the social science that studies human behavior in society's material setting, including the production, distribution, and consumption of goods and services, for the purpose of using choice, and allocative and productive efficiency, to overcome the human condition of scarcity.*

CENTURIES OF DEVELOPMENT: A STEP BACK IN TIME

- *Social Sciences developed in the 18th and 19th Centuries.*
- *Formal lines and rules of thought and inquiry were created in studies of human behavior. Studies of human behavior became social sciences such as economics, sociology, and political science.*
- *Political economics, a precursor of economics, emerged from an interest in national wealth by the Physiocrats of France and Adam Smith in Great Britain.*
- *The national concept of wealth changed from the accumulation of monetarized metals to the increase in productivity of a nation's workers.*
- *The study of economics emerged by shedding the "Political" title and focusing on the moral purpose of increasing citizen welfare and well-being.*

- *Economics of the 20th Century incorporated advanced mathematical analysis and model building to improve the study of economic efficiency to address the problem of scarcity.*

ECONOMICS: A SHORT STORY OF A SOCIAL SCIENCE

"The ultimate purpose of economics, of course, is to understand and promote the enhancement of well-being."

---Ben Bernanke

ECONOMICS: A SOCIAL SCIENCE

As a professor, sometimes students ask me, "Why should I choose Economics as my college course?" In fact, this first draft's title was "Why Study Economics?". People in my social circles ask me to give them economic advice. To establish better communication, I start by telling them *what economics is not*. It tightens the conversation. So first, the "not" part.

The *social science of economics* is not a course in finance. Nor is it a course on investment planning, nor playing in speculative markets like stocks, crypto-coin, real estate, gold, or product futures. It is not a study of business management or procedures. These areas move economics into more specialized subareas and insert economists into various occupations. Economists may work for government agencies studying economic data or developing economic forecasts for economic growth and monetary policies. Economists also may work for investment houses to make recommendations for buying and selling financial products. Economists may often work for research institutes of data creation, analysis, and interpretation. They may be employed by corporations to improve the productive efficiency of a company's internal organization, supply chains, automation, technology, communication, transportation, or management techniques. Economists are hired as consultants for the law and medical professions and for businesses. Economists may be professors at colleges and universities.

These occupations show economists in action but do not define economics. *Economics is a social science that studies human behavior in society's material setting, including the production, distribution, and consumption of goods and services, for the purpose of using choice, and productive and allocative efficiencies, to overcome the human condition of scarcity.*

CENTURIES OF DEVELOPMENT: A STEP BACK IN TIME

After building on the humanism of the Renaissance, the Age of Enlightenment began in the late 17th Century Europe with the advancement of human reasoning's ability to understand the world and mankind's place in it. By the 18th Century, intellectuals expanded this advancement into the ideas of morality, progress, liberty, and the scientific method, as well, as areas of society, politics, and the economy. Denis Diderot and Jean le Roul d'Alembert, along with contributions of one hundred fifty other intellectuals, began an ambitious writing project to include all of mankind's knowledge. It resulted in an encyclopedia published between 1751 and 1772. This burst of intellectual energy seeded what became the social sciences.

In the middle of the 18th Century, a group of French philosophers known as Physiocrats, associated with Francois Quesnay, began studying the question of national wealth. It was timely because European nations were competing for global power and colonial wealth. The national wealth question soon moved to Great Britain. Social sciences were developed during this century under the study of moral philosophy, and it was under that study that Adam Smith[1] assumed the position of professor at the University of Glasgow. He was part of the Scottish Enlightenment. His second book, *An Inquiry into the Nature and Causes of The Wealth of Nations* in 1776, organized the existing thinking on the question of national wealth, but its insight became the foundation of modern economics. The book argued against the mercantilist preference for government control and power. It laid out a more democratic economic plan of national wealth based on employees' specialization, abilities, and proper education. Smith proposed a moral and more satisfying participation in a democratic community. His concept of national wealth was not based on Mercantilist ideas of trade protection and hoarding gold and silver. Rather, Smith explained that national wealth would increase through workers' productivity, production efficiency, job specialization, and business competition under market conditions. Society would repel avarice with the moral structure and well-being of what he called the plentitude of the perfect society ("economics" was not yet its designation). Controlled self-interest would unleash national wealth. The dynamic operation of the marketplace would diminish government control of economic activity. Even though his thoughts coincided with anti-imperialism, they were not influential enough to change the failed British policy toward the American colonies. But his economic ideas have influenced intellectuals for centuries.

Smith's *Wealth of Nations* expanded his theme of moral philosophy, but, in the early 19th Century, this theme spawned a new area of study, Political Economy, that continued to explore sources of national wealth and power. It developed economic policies more focused on individuals' roles instead of governmental roles. Contributors who took up the challenge included Thomas Malthus, John Stuart Mill, and David Riccardo. They explored ideas such as labor wages, markets, and international trade, respectively. Economists advanced market demand and supply equilibrium theory for general economic application. A mathematical school of Marginalists, led by Willaim Henry Jevons, pursued their theories without the assumptions of political power and settings of classes and privilege. The economist, Alfred Marshall, buried the reference to "political" with his publication of the widely used textbook, *Principles of Economics* (1890). The textbook codified mathematical analysis to the narrower study of economics, establishing what the economist Paul Samuelson later called the Queen of the Social Sciences. Economic theory became not just discursive narration and argumentation, but a mathematically based science. Marshall was philosophically and socially concerned with Smith's moral notion of improving citizens' lives and national wealth.

The 20th Century increased mathematical applications that crowned economics as first among the social sciences. Various branches of economics developed[2]. In 1968, economics was designated as the Nobel Memorial Prize in Economic Sciences and became the only social science of the six Nobel Prizes.[3] Classical economists, Keynesian economists, Monetarists, and Marxist economists coexisted, while Behavioral economists looked further into the behavior of human beings to explain an economy. After World War II, economic metrics and data collection were created to monitor national economic activity. Data drew statistical fields around such concepts as Gross Domestic Product, unemployment, international trade, and inflation. Following Keynesian economic theory, federal government's entities such as the Federal Reserve Bank, the Commerce Department, the Bureau of Economic Analysis, the Bureau of Labor Statistics, and the Census Bureau used data compilation and analysis to guide management of the economy. The influence of Keynesian theory resulted in the Full Employment Act of 1946, which provided for the monitoring of economic growth to steer clear of the dangers of inflation and recessionary (cyclical) unemployment. It also ensured the working public a right to full employment.

Twenty-first Century economists do not always agree on economic policies, but they seem to coalesce around an amalgam of neoclassical and Keynesian theory. They continue to honor economics' moral purpose of addressing scarcity issues of poverty, income inequality, poor health care, and adequate living conditions. Advanced economic theory and mathematics continues to champion ethical purpose, economic freedom, and democratic institutions.

CHAPTER 3

HIGHLIGHTS

THE AMERICAN EXPERIENCE

- *Capitalism is an economic system in which the factors of production are privately owned, and individual owners of capital are free to make use of it for profit.*
- *American Capitalism has four key characteristics:*
    1. *sanctity of private property and ownership of productive capacity,*
    2. *economic freedom,*
    3. *existence of competitive markets, and*
    4. *legal protection of contracts and commerce.*

- *American Capitalism is a mixture of capitalism and socialism.*
- *Governments in the United States account for about 25% of national income.*
- *American Capitalism was created pragmatically over centuries through provisions of the U.S. Constitution and subsequent legal specifications.*
- *The existing strengths and weaknesses of the nation's Constitution and laws provide the political framework for our mission.*

AMERICAN CAPITALISM: FINDING COMMON GROUND

"It is no crime to be ignorant of economics, which is, after all, a specialized discipline and one that most people consider to be a 'dismal science.' But it is totally irresponsible to have a loud and vociferous opinion on economic subjects while remaining in this state of ignorance."

--Murray N. Rothbard

"The way to maximize production is to maximize the incentives to production. And the way to do that, as the modern world has discovered, is through the system known as capitalism—the system of private property, free markets, and free enterprise."

-- Henry Hazlitt

THE AMERICAN EXPERIENCE

The Oxford Dictionary defines *capitalism* as "an economic system in which the factors of production are privately owned, and individual owners of capital are free to make use of it as they see fit; in particular, for their own profit."

The American system of capitalism exhibits four key characteristics:

- *sanctity of private property and ownership of productive capacity*
- *economic freedom*
- *existence of competitive markets, and*
- *legal protection of contracts and commerce.*

American Capitalism is a variant of a more theoretical capitalist system of minimal government participation. The American economy, however, is a mixed economy of capitalism and socialism. According to the United States Treasury (2022), about 75% of economic activity was in private ownership (capitalist) and about 25% was in government control and ownership (socialist). The socialist sector includes ownership and legal involvement of federal, state, and local governments. States and towns maintain the likes of public education, public roads, public utilities, police forces, sidewalks, libraries, land for governmental buildings, playgrounds, and courts. Additionally, the federal government's Executive Branch controls the nation's military forces and national guard (with the states). The United States government owns about 29% of the country's land area. It runs federal agencies and indirectly influences the nation's economy through Congressional budgeting, its connection to the Federal Reserve Bank of the United States, and regulated government-sponsored enterprises such as the mortgage companies of Freddie Mac and Fannie Mae. State and federal governments employ about 27.3 million civilian and military people.

The American public and government have taken a pragmatic route to expand the economy, sometimes depending on the marketplace, and sometimes using government involvement for the public good.

American Capitalism was forged out of a revolution over the rights of Great Britain's thirteen North America colonies in the mid-eighteenth century. Taxation, economic and political freedom, and trade rights surfaced as central issues that led to open revolt. Once the former colonies were established as an independent nation, its second and current government was formed under the United States Constitution in 1789.

European Enlightenment Philosophers[1] of the 18th Century influenced the Founding Fathers' pursuit of fashioning a democratic government that would protect land and business rights. The U.S. Constitution outlined a mixture of private economic rights and public responsibilities for economic activity. A Bill of Rights was added to the original document to delineate and protect state and citizen rights. Over the last two and one-third centuries, a total of twenty-seven amendments have been added, as well as a legal structure fashioned by legislative/executive law creation and judiciary review.

Looking at the American economy's success, we see that it was largely made possible by the private sector's profit-seeking motive. American capitalism became characterized by corporations that have the legal designation as "person" to make contracts, hold property, and have standing in courts' legal proceedings. Over the country's history, they have continued to wield economic power in production, retail and wholesale pricing, investments, and labor wage markets. A few powerful corporations inhabit many industries including food, auto, airline, manufacturing, pharmacology, health, entertainment, mass media, petroleum, military-industrial defense, technology, and telecom.

Private and public interests are balanced by the powers of business and government and are informed by the social science of economics. Corporations conduct their activities for shareholders' profit. Top corporate management receives high compensation to maximize it. Along the way, short shrift has been given to social cohesion, environmental sustainability, and citizen well-being. These are not normal to business plans and calculations, but they are normal in economics' moral purposes of promoting national and citizen success. Citizens' well-being resides in the United States Constitution's Preamble, where the fifth reason for its establishment is *to promote the general welfare.*

The history of American Capitalism is an uneven one of establishing corporate rights, protecting citizen rights, or expanding minority and gender groups to full citizenship. A desire for a more perfect union is how the Preamble to the Constitution puts it. *A more perfect union must involve decreasing citizens' Econ-Angst while increasing economic hopes.*

Becoming familiar with relevant civil rights and responsibilities is necessary for citizenship in general. Interest groups that perceive inequities in civil and economic rights use tools such as lockouts, tariffs, income redistribution taxation, boycotts, strikes, laws, and economic demonstrations. Individual citizens will likely be drawn into larger social, economic, and political issues. Mechanisms of power politics overlay an individual's Econ-Angst, but addressing these political struggles is not explored here. Suffice it to say that the existing biases, struggles, strengths, and weaknesses of the nation's Constitution and laws provide the framework for our mission. The field of economics is our focus.

CHAPTER 4

HIGHLIGHTS

DEFINING ECONOMICS AS A SOCIAL SCIENCE

- *Economics is a social science that studies the provision systems for material life and their economic actions within it.*
- *Economics is divided into two parts: Macroeconomics and Microeconomics.*

TWO CENTRAL CONCEPTS

- *Economics takes as its central mission the mitigation of the human and social conditions of scarcity.*
- *Two pillars of economics*
- *The existence of the human and social conditions of scarcity.*

- *The competition for resource and allocative efficiencies.*

THE RELATIONSHIP BETWEEN SCARCITY AND EFFICIENCY

- *The Scarcity-Efficiency Tension (SET)*

ECONOMICS DEFINED: TWO KEY CONCEPTS

"Economics is everywhere, and understanding economics can help you make better decisions and lead a happier life."

--Tyler Cowen

DEFINING ECONOMICS AS A SOCIAL SCIENCE

Economics has been described as a social science that studies people's provision systems for material life and their economic actions within it. It is a study of human characteristics and behavior working within a system that provides for life's material wants and needs.

There are other descriptions coming from different views.

- *"Economics is a social science that focuses on the production, distribution, and consumption of goods and services, and analyzes the choices that individuals, businesses, governments, and nations make to allocate resources". -- Investopia*

- *"Economics is the science that studies how people and societies make decisions that allow them to get the most out of their limited resources. Because every country, every business, and every person deal with constraints and limitations, economics is literally everywhere." -- Economics for Dummies.*

- *"Economy is the art of making the most of life."*

  --George Bernard Shaw

- *"Economics is the study of mankind in the ordinary business of life."*

  --Alfred Marshall.

- *"Economics . . . is the philosophy of human life and action and concerns everybody and everything. It is the pith of civilization and of man's human existence."*

  --Ludwig Von Mises

- *"The theory of economics is a method rather than a doctrine, an apparatus of mind, a technique of thinking, which helps its possessor to draw correct conclusions."*

  --John Maynard Keynes

This social science has two vantage points. One is from the national (or global) level and is called *Macroeconomics*. Macroeconomics examines aggregated (total) economic activities of a nation's employment, production, prices, and growth. The second vantage point is from a partial and segmented level of economic activity. It examines the business of life at a level of industries, firms, markets, or the consumer. It is called *Microeconomics*.

TWO CENTRAL CONCEPTS

Economics' foundation has two conceptual pillars--*scarcity* and *efficiency*.

Economics takes as a central mission the mitigation of the human and social conditions of scarcity. It is economics' first foundational pillar. Economists view scarcity exists when human wants and needs are greater than the ability of resources to provide for them. If all necessary resources (including lifetimes) were infinite, there would be no need for the study of economics. But there is scarcity that haunts society and its citizens: the scarcity of natural resources, human resources, machine capital, and technology.

Examples of scarcity occur when a child goes to an expensive internet toy site as well as when a newlywed couple enters a real estate site. Wants and needs can surpass what is affordable. This also occurs at a macroeconomic level when satisfying countries' needs and wants is beyond national resources. Economists refer to this as the "guns or butter" budgeting dilemma. It exists when countries lack resources to cover both military costs and domestic costs. At a global level, the earth's population has increasingly realized that there is an existential scarcity of earth resources for both ecological health and human population.

Having placed *scarcity* as a central condition of humanity, economics responds with the second foundational pillar, the concept of *efficiency.* Efficiency means finding the optimum use of resources needed to satisfy human wants and needs at the personal, social, and global levels. Efficiency is needed at the production level (microeconomic cost efficient) and at the resource level (macroeconomic allocation efficient). Achieving these efficiencies effects roles and functions within the economic system. In this way, economics becomes a teaching science for citizens, companies, and governments when making choices.

THE RELATIONSHIP BETWEEN SCARCITY AND EFFICIENCY

People will undoubtedly partake economic roles such as consumer, business owner, inventor, employee, investor, employer, retiree, or student. But in any case, roles must be learned and established while using economic resources. Economic efficiencies are necessary to prevent resource over-use. A dynamic relationship occurs between scarcity and efficiency, the *Scarcity-Efficiency Tension (SET).* The tension is anxiety created when efficient technologies, behaviors, and programs cannot keep pace with scarcity. It occurs at governmental, company, or personal levels. Earth's resource scarcity occurs in rare earth minerals, industrial metals, and non-renewable energy sources; but clean air, clean water, and agricultural land are the headliners. Global efficiency tools are needed for that trio. Corporations, as well as the United Nations and regional organizations, will have to act to lessen the SET. An individual citizen must live according to efficiency tools. Households must be run with efficiency. This would include utility usage, care of appliances and furnishings, car usage, coordination of activities, and smart shopping choices. Otherwise, SET will increase, and Econ-Angst will deepen.

SET has increased over the 20th Century's industrial revolution with a growing gap between impending scarcity and efficiency. In the 21st Century, factors of world population growth and the spread of "dirty" economic activities have pushed scarcity toward unsustainable levels. Controlling SET depends upon improved efficiency measures of production, technology application, resource usage, and population behaviors. It also depends on the proper allocation (choices) of where to dedicate resources within the economy. *Economic activities must be judged by the effect on SET.*

Addressing SET could be called "thinking outside the box." But, with an understanding of key economic concepts, it is called, "expanding the size of the box." For example, the energy industry accounts for three-quarters of air pollution while creating the energy for economies, however, they also make clean air scarcer each year. The International Energy Agency (IEA) has established a goal of net zero emissions by 2050. Net zero emissions refers to reducing greenhouse gas emissions as close to zero as possible. Renewable energy industries of solar, wind, geothermal, hydroelectric, bioenergy, and ocean wave-and-current are working to reduce dependence on non-renewable fossil fuels to meet the 2050 calendar goal. SET will be reduced by increased efficiency and reduction of scarce resource usage. The challenge is for countries and their citizens to stay on the IEA's track. The United States and China are two of the most global culprits.

SET is a barometer check for an economy, an industry, a firm, and a citizen. It can inform sustainability concerns for firms and governmental agencies when making important economic decisions. It is a valuable mark for individuals' decisions about economic choices. It is a part of the markings that are needed to ease the emotional hardships of Econ-Angst.

CHAPTER 5

HIGHLIGHTS

ECONOMIC CAIRNS

- *Economic Cairns are economic markers that ease SET and Econ-Angst along life's economic journey.*
- *Economic Cairns' purpose is to apply economic intelligence to create a less stressful path to well-being.*

ECONOMIC FREEDOM'S DUAL NATURE

- *Increased opportunities and inequitable opportunities*
- *Increased rights and responsibilities*

THE TEN ECONOMIC CAIRNS: INTRODUCTION

- *Economic freedom provides opportunities.*

- *Opportunities introduce and aggravate SET.*
- *SET contributes to Econ-Angst.*
- *Economic Cairns ease Econ-Angst.*

EASING ECON-ANGST: ECONOMIC CAIRNS

"It's a dangerous business, Frodo, going out your door. You step onto the road, and if you don't keep your feet, there's no knowing where you might be swept off to."

– J.R.R. Tolkien, The Lord of the Rings.

A Scottish cairn to guide the foot traveler.

ECONOMIC CAIRNS

Stones pile markers, called Cairns (pronounced *kehrnz*), are common trail markers in the Scottish Highlands and other parts of the world. While visiting Scotland, I came across the use of stone piles to reassure trekkers about the journey's correct direction. Cairns were symbols that eased the insecurity of the path forward. This gave birth to the idea of *Economic Cairns*: *economic markers that ease SET and Econ-Angst along life's economic journey.* Economic Cairns mitigate citizens' anxiety while striving for success. They provide points of economic intelligence for the challenging decisions of consumer purchasing, jobs and occupations, education and schooling, locations to live and work, when to marry or partner, and investment risk-taking. They can inform decisions regarding the problem of scarcity and implementation of efficiency that enhance a sense of well-being. *Economic Cairns' purpose is to apply economic intelligence to create a less stressful path to well-being.*

ECONOMIC FREEDOM'S DUAL NATURE

The record of American economic freedom has led to unparalleled economic success. It has led to a vast array of available educational, personal, and occupational paths and experiences. Keys to American economic freedom include protection of private property rights, judicial effectiveness, labor union membership, banking and investment opportunities, and government integrity and regulation. There is little political consensus on their operation. A debate exists between liberal positions of the economic safety net and conservative positions of less government interference in the economy. But these are political and ideological positions. You don't want to learn economics from politicians and special interest ideologues. They have their reasons. Your best interest is not one of them.

We need to stay more to the point. Americans' economic freedom comes with a sense of insecurity in a search for well-being. There are well-known insecurities about employment, consumer prices, tax rates, housing costs, utility costs, and transportation costs. The capitalist stressors of unemployment and inflation weave through life.

The 20th Century's sense of semi-permanent job positions has given way to a lack of trust that accelerates the labor-management disconnect. Jobs that once seemed necessary to corporations and governments have been subcontracted, outsourced, and moved out of state or country. Ever-changing modern production functions and inputs have displaced traditional employment and job security. Companies, in the drive for efficiency and profits, continue to move production out of the country and replace employees with automated machinery, technological improvements, and digitalized communications and software programs. On the employee side of the employment contract, workers' locational movements and job jumping have eroded company's loyalty. The new century has increased job insecurity by loosening the employment contract connection between employer and employee.

Economic freedom does not come without cost. It requires a foundation of personal and socially responsible behavior. Its ride is not well marked; it is not guaranteed; it is not certain; rather, it must be planned and earned. Economic freedom carries stressors that create Econ-Angst. Along life's journey, constant worry abounds with a sudden loss of income and wealth, illness or death of family members, weather-related catastrophes, cyclical layoffs, structural unemployment, or aging out of skills and abilities.

Economic freedom has, unfortunately, not been equitably experienced in the United States. Economic outcomes continue to be enhanced or diminished by the circumstance of location or accident of birth; not everyone starts on third base. Many must earn their way to the batter's box. Gender, racial, and ethnic factors bring inequities to life's starting points and outcomes. Recent south-of-the-border immigrants, as well as minorities of color, continue to underperform in education, wealth attainment, and earnings. Women's earnings, generally and in the same job positions, continue to lag men's pay. Social and economic biases place citizens at different starting points and harder paths. These are not of their making. However, no matter what circumstances or paths traveled, *Economic Cairns* can ease the Econ-Angst and enhance well-being. But before using *Economic Cairns*, time must be dedicated to understanding them.

Economic freedom provides opportunities. Opportunities introduce and aggravate SET. SET increases Econ-Angst. Economic Cairns ease Econ-Angst.

THE TEN ECONOMIC CAIRNS: INTRODUCTION

Centuries of economic growth and increased market freedoms have improved life for much of the world's population. Capitalist and democratic concepts have led nations on the road to becoming materially advanced, healthier, and happier. The good news is that similar economic concepts contained in *Economic Cairns* can be applied to gaining personal improvement by diminishing Econ-Angst. A full explanation of the ten Economic Cairns is included in Chapter VI. *Building a stone cairn on a hillside takes thought, time, and energy. So does building an understanding of an Economic Cairn.*

CHAPTER 6

HIGHLIGHTS

THE TEN ECONOMIC CAIRNS

1. USING SELF-KNOWLEDGE ECO-SELF PERSPECTIVES

   Experiencing your ***eco-self*** *and your place and path in the new economy.*

2. ADDRESSING THE SCARCITY PROBLEM

   Understanding the effect of finite resources; ***Scarcity-Efficiency Tension (SET).***

3. *PROMOTING ECONOMIC COMPETITION+*

   Replacing winning and greed with **Economic Competition+.**

4. *RECOGNIZING OPPORTUNITY COSTS*

   Facing that "Nothing is free". Overcoming ***naïve economics****.*

5. *USING MARGINAL ANALYSIS*

    Step-by-step decision-making at the margins.

6. *LIVING BY A NEW WORK ETHIC*

    Realizing there is no easy way. Combating the ***fantasy economy.***

7. *INVESTING IN YOURSELF*

    Calculating the payout of formal and informal education.

8. *BRANDING YOURSELF*

    Constructing "you as the product."

9. *REALIZING THE ONLY CONSTANT IS CHANGE*

    Knowing the pace of change. "Tomorrow is this morning."

10. *MAKING EFFICIENT LIFE CHOICES*

    Learning by doing. Following the markers.

THE TEN ECONOMIC CAIRNS

"If we wanted to change the situation, we first had to change ourselves. And to change ourselves effectively, we first had to change our perceptions."

- Stephen Covey

CAIRN 1: USING SELF-KNOWLEDGE ECO-SELF PERSPECTIVES

"The purpose of education is to turn mirrors into windows."

- Sydney J. Harris

Self-knowledge is an area of study developed over the years by philosophers, sociologists, and psychologists. As such, it has various aspects with roots found in logical-mathematical, intrapersonal, interpersonal, and emotional intelligences. However, for our purpose, self-knowledge speaks to the mind's openness to experience oneself from multiple dimensions and perspectives of and within the economic world. Economists study human behavior in the business of life. They give two unique perspectives of yourself in an economy. One economic perspective is a mirror assessment of who you are: looking at your knowledge base, skill set, and learning ability. The second perspective is out a window view of the economic landscape. This perspective sees economic possibilities and opportunities.

Looking in the mirror and out the window at the same time develops a beneficial economic perspective. Knowing present abilities, economic settings, and opportunities increases motivation for improvement, continued education, and self-promotion. It lets you polish your learning IQ[1]. It expands the concept of yourself to include your work-self or business-self. This is your economic self, shortened to *eco-self.* Eco-self functions as more than a work personality. It is that good friend who knows you best, calms you down, and advises you for success. Cairn

1 increases the freedom and openness to better see and advise yourself while adding value to your economic life. Eco-self is grounded and content to be involved with others in the economy. It has the self-confidence to interact in the economy and see better opportunities.

Economists look at individual and group behavior in an economy. They view the characteristics of the individual as well as the characteristics of the economy. Individuals find themselves in markets for labor, management, consumer goods, producer goods, or investments. The eco-self needs to have the flexibility to function in multiple corners and levels of the economy. It must have the dynamic to adjust views in the mirror and out the window.

Economists place individuals within the larger picture of the nation (or world). Economists organize economic data by macro groupings to study the economy. They identify socio-economic classes--upper, middle, or lower. They identify individuals as socially mobile, unemployed, owners, or labor. There are age identifications by birth years: the Silent Generation,1928-1945; Baby Boomers,

1946-1964; Generation X,1965-1980; Millennials, 1981-1996; Generation Z,1997-2012; and Generation A, 2013 and beyond. Each generation has consumer and employment characteristics along with cultural identifications of style, music, icons, and jargon. Other demographic groupings are used, including immigration, generation order, ethnic identification, race, family birth order, education level, and gender. Citizens identify with these groupings, and the setting influences eco-self. Individuals reflect grouping identifications to construct their eco-self within the economy.

Identifications and memberships are uplifting and necessary for eco-self's knowledge. Eco-self's freedom of economic life is seen as the staging platform for growth. But over-reliance on group identification can act as concrete of action, stifling the agility needed in a dynamic economy. The comfort of your group's identification may not always be your best friend.

Eco-self involves the flexibility to see and experience yourself from above and taking stock of your place in the world from 30,000 feet—a kind of out-of-body experience. This perspective is an exercise in taking the time to assess self-awareness.

- *Who do you see?*
- *What behaviors?*
- *What skills and knowledgeable actions?*
- *What values?*
- *What is lacking?*
- *Are you taking full advantage of your knowledge and skills?*
- *Do you have a planned path toward success?*

It is experiencing yourself in the time and place of your personal history. Sometimes, we get lost in day-to-day immediate attentions. But you can "get over yourself" from 30,000 feet. This is where you can monitor wider employment and locational opportunities instead of seeing what is just in front.

Cairn 1 describes the flexibility of the mind's eco-self to take advantage of experiences and plan for a better place in the economy. It eases Econ-Angst by developing a wider mental picture of the economic system and a moving timeframe toward future goals. Knowing what you are doing in the short term is necessary; life's steps need the awareness of immediate attention. But a longer-term awareness of time and space is also necessary; the steps of life also need the perspective of reflective thought to travel the road ahead. The comic Rodney Dangerfield put it this way, *"Look out for number one . . . but don't step in number two."*

Being a time shifter, so to speak, can experience life in multiple dimensions and roles at the same time. A worker can act as her supervisor; an actor can also be a director; an athlete can be her own trainer; or a tourist can act as the guide. These dynamic and synchronous views create openness to possibilities of advancement and goal accomplishment.

Economic intelligence gives an omnibus mental picture of life within the structure of the economy by concentrating on the current job but visualizing an economic future. Eco-self's mind keeps thinking about future jobs and occupations, locale, skills, and educational advancement. Eco-self asks questions:

- *What if the job will no longer be needed?*
- *What is the horizon of this career's existence?*
- *Is your business in a growth sector or a vanishing sector of the economy?*
- *How does the path ahead affect loved ones?*
- *How best is it to navigate a developing and changing employment or business picture?*
- *Where am I going to be on the two-year horizon or on the five-year horizon?*
- *Isn't the best time to plan and look for a better job while you have one?*

Visualizing or dreaming of an employment future is part of the first Cairn.

Economists assume people to be rational actors in the economy who act in self-interest to attain well-being (however, Behavioral Economists may not always agree). This Cairn uses the rational actor assumption to a limited extent, but also sees the rational actor with a passionate side. Making economic decisions must be a balance of thought and emotion. Calculating positives and negatives has a place, but so do feelings of connection to family, friends, and social groups. Rational and emotional parts combine to form heightened self-awareness that increases eco-self's knowledge. Cairn 1 marks the economic path by expanding awareness of the immediate position or place within the microeconomy while anticipating changes in the macroeconomy.

Looking out the window and past the media noise needs to focus on the corner of the economy you inhabit. But it is necessary to also assemble useful economic data and knowledge. They can be accessed on academic, non-profit, neutral organizations, or government websites.

- *The Bureau of Labor Statistics (see Appendix) keeps a list of declining occupations in various parts of the economy.*

- *Organizations and companies are peering into the future job requirements and needs for the future to 2030[2]. They predict major changes in employment skills and company environments. There will be 20th Century-type job losses and also comparable increases in technology and Green (pro-environment) jobs. Most jobs will be either eliminated or revamped, including taxi drivers, truck drivers, cashiers, teachers, and data entry clerks. New jobs will be available such as applications developers, drone pilots, or virtual reality specialists. Various existing employment positions will undergo dramatic skill and knowledge changes even if the position stays the same.*

- *Career Addict*[3] *listed U.S. jobs that will be disappearing by 2030. They identified fifteen jobs including travel agents, fast food cooks and employees, mail carriers, bank tellers, textile workers, telemarketers, lumber jacks, professional fishers, and legal secretaries.*
- *The World Economic Forum*[4] *consists of over 800 companies that meet annually in Davos, Switzerland. It publishes a report that discusses future areas of risks to the nations and citizens of the world at two-year and ten-year horizons. It assesses categories of economic, geopolitical, environmental, technological, and social changes.*

For additional economic perspectives, there are government and professional sites that are available, such as

- *the Conference Board,*
- *the Congressional Budget Office,*
- *the International Monetary Fund,*
- *the Federal Reserve Bank,*

- *the Organisation for Economic Co-operation and Development (OECD), and*
- *many large private banks and financial companies.*

Important large-scale factors of employment and quality of life occur at the world level. The global perspective of dangers and successes provides a seat to view economic trends and shifts.

History was made by the Bureau of Labor Statistics in May 2023 when it published the first unemployment numbers created by Artificial Intelligence (AI). No doubt AI will create new job categories and increase efficiency in many others, but it also will diminish employment elsewhere. The concern over AI is creating one of the critical questions of the 21st Century. But at this time, it is more of a concern for Millennials, Gen Zs, and Gen As, whose jobs may be negatively affected for mid-management, teachers, legal paraprofessionals, market analysts, financial advisers, translators, web designers, lawyers, coders, accountants, copywriters, or human resource professionals.

Macro-factors, known or unknown, lay the table for how changes may impact citizens. Each of the risks will filter down to street and work level depending upon a worker's place in the economy; for example, new energy source applications may change sectors and corporate organizations that will disrupt employment work skills and categories. Cairn 1 eases Econ-Angst by anticipating new employment opportunities that will increase job efficiency.

A look into the future lacks the clarity of today, but anticipating economic change is part of economic intelligence. Economists predict future economic changes, but their tea leaves and crystal balls are no better than the data fed into them. Past performance is no guarantee of future performance, but seeing into the foggy future is better than being blind.

Cairn 1's eco-self sees you in the mirror and you as a participant in the economy. It is both wide and long, including a larger view of today's, along with tomorrow's, place in the economy. Expanding the economic landscape, lengthening its horizon, and imagining its dynamic brings a calming sense of belonging within the system. *Cairn 1 eases Econ-Angst through the empowerment of experiencing yourself in two perspectives and by deepening economic knowledge now and anticipating economic conditions later.*

CAIRN 2: ADDRESSING THE SCARCITY PROBLEM

"If every day were Earth Day, we wouldn't be in the mess we're in."

--Neil deGrasse Tyson.

"We are the first generation to feel the impact of climate change and the last generation that can do something about it."

--Barack Obama

Social sciences study the social nature and interactive environment of humans (think psychology, sociology, economics, anthropology, or demography), while physical sciences study the physical nature of the earth and universe (think biology, chemistry, physics, or astronomy). As social scientists then, economists study human behaviors and interactions in markets and economic systems to improve well-being and standards of living. Its primary postulate is that humans need and want more than can be provided. Humans appear to never be satisfied because their needs and wants are unlimited. But they also recognize that humans live in a world of finite resources, traditionally called land, labor, and capital. The land resource refers to what it grown on and available under the ground, such as agricultural acreage, forests, oil, or industrial metal ores. The labor resource refers to the number of workers and their skills and knowledge. Capital refers to the physical technology and machinery necessary to produce goods and services in the economy. *It does not refer to financial capital.* These finite resources have a limited ability to meet needs and wants. The conflict between humans' unlimited needs and wants and limited resources creates the economic concept of *scarcity*. Just as family resources face a limit, the resource footprint needed to sustain the earth's population faces an existential limit.

Technological advances have cleared the way forward in previous centuries, but there may be a limit to the inventiveness and ingenuity of humans this time. Past technologies that were answers to production scarcity have now become environmental problems for the new century (witness the combustible engine). So, is it possible for the planet's resources to satisfy 10 million people? The question needs an answer probably before 2050. *The world's economic activity has a scarcity and sustainability problem.*

UNDERSTANDING EFFICIENCY

The economic concept of scarcity impacts both individual decisions, social decisions, and public decisions. Economics' response to this scarcity problem lies in the concept of *efficiency*. There are two aspects to efficiency, one is productive efficiency, and the other is allocative efficiency. Productive efficiency means getting the greatest output for each unit input. Examples would be most shoes produced per worker, most corn produced per acre, or most cars produced per factory. Allocative efficiency means using resources to produce the most valuable (wanted) goods and services—the greatest value per amount of resource. Examples would be using metal resources to produce automobiles rather than carriages or using technology to produce computers rather than electric typewriters. Consumer demand would determine allocative efficiency in the market. Government decisions would determine allocative efficiency for public needs and wants.

Economists study and apply *efficiency* to the world's economic productive and consumptive activities. To focus on the study of efficiency, economists pose three questions: (1) what is to be produced; (2) how it is to be produced; and (3) for whom it is to be produced. Each economic system must answer these three questions.

Capitalism answers these questions in a democratic marketplace where consumers (questions #1, #3) and businesses (#2) are the prime decision-makers.

There are guard rails to the lane which economists travel. It is the foundational moral value to improve human well-being while creating national wealth. Waste, both individual and societal, is the enemy of economic efficiency.

The new economic citizenship plays an important part in efficiency. The 20th Century's throw-away and replace-don't-repair behaviors must be reversed to combat scarcity. Human resources are wasted when limits and barriers are placed on citizens' education, talents, opportunities, and potential. This is especially true for minority groups and gender. Inefficiency costs deepen SET and increases Econ-Angst. The goal of efficiency is a necessary part of economic citizenship. More efficient behavior must be practiced as a consumer and worker.

Businesses, organizations, and governments provide leaders who have the challenge of managing society's scarcity problem within their green-planning and efficient decisions of productive efficiency. They must also consider allocative inefficiency as social and environmental costs. Damage occurs to society and the environment when productive resources are misallocated. Companies' internal costs do not cover the social costs of air and water pollution, and the indirect population healthcare costs. The new economic citizenship must call for responsibility to the earth and human quality of life. Economic competition must tally the winners and losers within the economy.

Economic growth contributes to irregulated pollution around the world. The 21st Century economy must create an efficient feedback loop of environmental and social costs to the point of pollution. There is an answer to the pollution problem by sharing the costs of clean up. Social and environmental costs of production can be paid in four ways; (1) through increased consumer prices, (2) paid through lower corporate profits, (3) paid by government budgeting and taxation arrangements, or (4) paid according to some combination of each.

Direct and targeted costs are beginning to be estimated. There have been attempts to calculate the direct-damage costs of carbon emissions to the environment. The U.S. Environmental Protections Agency (March 9, 2023) and the *Nature Journal* (September 1, 2022) have given the damage cost of carbon emissions released into the atmosphere at $190/ton and $185/ton of carbon, respectively (up from earlier estimates). According to *Chemical and Engineering News* (August 25, 2023), covering this additional social cost for corporations would reduce profits by an average of 44%. Another climate threat gas, Methane, has a social cost to the environment that would be multiples higher. Other groups such as Earth.org, Stanford University, Columbia University's Climate School, Resources for the Future, Institute for Policy Integrity (The Cost of Carbon), The Environmental Defense Fund, The Carbon Disclosure Project, The Intergovernmental Panel on Climate Change, The Global Footprint Network, Carbon

Brief, Clear on Climate, Tradewater, and ClimateXchange have missions to address climate costs and damages.

Behind the logos and name plates of powerful leaders in business and government, these individuals must hold up their responsibilities of the new economic citizenship. The parameters of their decisions may be different than those of the average American, but the social and environmental responsibilities are the same, and, given their lofty positions, may even be heavier to bear.

Their last century's economic citizenship attitudes are improving. Businesses and governments are increasing their recognition of the new economic citizenship's responsibility. The French carbon-tracking organization *Greenly* has a Carbon Footprint Tracker (2023) service showing over 1000 companies that have reduced greenhouse emissions. British Petroleum-USA supports the federal regulation of methane emissions from new and existing sources. The August 2019 *Fortune* magazine identified 101 companies committed to reducing their carbon footprint in the fields of agriculture, automobiles, travel, hospitality and restaurants, government, retail, manufacturing, software, construction, and innovation investments. Results have been spotty, with many plus-pollution companies and industries remaining. The U.S. Environmental Protection Agency and state departments of environment protection list and track information about toxic releases into the environment. The company *PwC* offers professional services to companies adjusting to the demands of the new economy in environmental and social governance.

Efforts of the federal and state governments have been directed toward green technologies. The federal government's 1970 National Environmental Policy Act has been strengthened in 2021 and 2022. The District of Columbia's Green Building Act (2006) required all non-residential buildings to meet higher environmental standards. The Energy Act 2020 promoted improved standards for the Environmental Protection Agencies' environmental footprint. The U.S. Census (2022) reported continued progress in federal and state spending for natural resource protections.

There is competition for earth's future between the private and government sectors. Which one is going to take the responsibility to lead the race for sustainability?

Governments and businesses plan for productive and allocative efficiencies through the budgeting process. However, individuals must be responsible for following the same budgeting process. Cairn 2 identifies three types of budgets for a household that need to be established: (1) for immediate financial demands; (2) for costs of medium length aims and goals; and (3) for the ability to dream and decide life issues. Budget One (weekly and cyclical) is needed for the immediate financial demands of utilities, shelter, food, and transportation. Budget Two (monthly and quarterly) is needed for the planning of medium aims and goals of health costs, credit card and note debts, vacation costs, or savings. Budget Three (process and yearly) is needed for longer-term dreams and major decisions of changes in employment, location, education or training, and family planning.

These budgets seem separate, but there is a dynamic interplay and overlay among them. Each one affects the others. The first budget may be the first in importance because of purchase choices. But what is spent daily, weekly, or monthly affects the money available for the other two. Depending on the employment picture, the third budget may be more important. The second budget could gain first place depending on health costs.

There are success stories of those who have managed SET when life's situations present themselves. Cairn 2 will limit Econ-Angst when SET grows in times of generational poverty, poor economic opportunities, life accidents, or personal misfortune. The three-budget plan and management will narrow the scarcity-efficiency gap and decrease SET in stressful times.

The severity of scarcity must not be viewed as a fateful condition but, rather, as a negative force to be challenged by discovering efficient resource usage and manner of life.

Just recognizing scarcity as a condition leaves little hope and much Econ-Angst. Using budgeting tools for economic efficiency will ease the path. Individuals of all economic roles have at their disposal the resources of energy, time, knowledge, skill, education, family and friend support, and smarts. Cairn 2 promotes using economic measurements to formulize efficiency and ease Econ-Angst while achieving a desired outcome.

WARNING MATHEMATICAL ANALYSIS!

Economists give *tools for efficiency*. Cairn 2 measures the efficiency of the desired ***o**utcome **p**er **r**esource unit (OPR)* much as car efficiency measures gas efficiency by miles per gallon (MPG).

1. Desired **o**utcome **p**er **e**nergy unit (OPE),
2. Desired **o**utcome **p**er **t**ime unit (OPT),
3. Desired **o**utcome **p**er **a**bility unit (OPA), or
4. Desired **o**utcome **p**er **d**ollar unit (OPD).

Households are economic parts of the economy and can be run similarly to governments and businesses. One way is to measure choices for outcomes by the input of the necessary resources. Think of output as valued items in the budgets. Think of input costs as available resource units. To accomplish your desired outcome, you want to know:

1. Output per unit of Energy (OPE)—how many physical and mental energy units (strength, stamina, clear-headedness, concentration) you can do (*Can I do it?),*

2. Output per unit of Time (OPT)—how many time units (hours in a day or week) do you have available (*Do I have time to do it?),*

3. Output per unit of Ability (OPA)—how many ability units (skill level, knowledge base) do you have (*Do I know how to do it?),* and

4. Output per unit of Dollar cost (OPD)—how many dollars (hiring help, outsourcing) does it cost (*Can I afford to do it?).*

Once measured in this way, individuals will create a personal and unique idea of the units for each resource. Thinking in units helps to focus on work and tasks making plans more concrete. When planning a to-do list, check your four efficiency measures so as not to waste their input. Do you know neighbors who left the bathroom renovation partially completed for four months? They had the ability (OPA) and energy (OPE) but may have run out of money (OPD) or run out of time (OPT).

Each measurement can be applied to a budget type or a budget line outcome to make the family unit more efficient. The efficiency is achieved by lowering waste for each budget's line outcome (the never-completed bathroom). Optimum allocation efficiency among outcome projects occurs when the resource-per-outcome value ratios are equal. If the outcome of fixing your daughter's bicycle is worth ten times doing the dinner dishes, then you can spend ten hours fixing the bicycle for every one hour doing the dishes. Both optimize your allocative efficiency.

10 value outcomes/10 hours = 1

which is the same as

1 value outcome/1 hour = 1,

so, 1=1.

Efficiency can mitigate scarcity and lower SET when each budget item outcome is at the lowest unit resource cost (OPR). Resources are optimally distributed when outcome per unit input ratios are equal within and among the three budgets.

ALL CLEAR

Budgeting across the income distribution of Americans will have different shapes and looks. American income and wealth inequality has been a recurrent characteristic of American Capitalism, and, by most measures, is higher now than at any time since World War II[5]. A family's place on the distribution, whether in the bottom 50% or the top 10%, will not change the efficiency strategy of budgeting, only the dollar numbers!

The scarcity problem exists for individuals as well as society. Addressing personal scarcity eases Econ-Angst by showing that economic life is not a permanent condition that we must passively accept. We must understand scarcity and the *tools for efficiency*. The American economy is not a movie we are watching. The new economic citizenship demands active participation in personal, societal, and environmental improvement. *American Capitalism is the stage where we decide what role we will play and how well we will play it.* Cairn 2 does not guarantee success but can make it easier by understanding economists' treatment of scarcity.

CAIRN 3: PROMOTING ECONOMIC COMPETITION+

"Whoever claims that economic competition represents survival of the fittest in the sense of the law of the jungle,

provides the clearest possible evidence of his lack of knowledge of economics."

--George Reisman.

The economic theory of competition is *not* the sports-type competition of determining *the* winner, *the* best in class, or the *top* cultural idol. The American culture has a fascination with winning. We celebrate winning in a competition with plaques, ribbons, trophies, flags, prize money, special privileges, and names etched on the "best of" list. This notion of competition is part of American exceptionalism. It shows up on bumper stickers: "Whoever dies with the most stuff wins." It shows up in movies: *War of the Roses*, "Yes, but I have more square footage." It shows up in media coverage of such events as the World Series, NCAA "March Madness," NHL and NBA finals, heavy-weight boxing championships, golf's The Masters, and the Olympic Gold Medal count. There is an identification with winning as exemplified by wearing team logos and by betting. Winning a bet makes one a winner even though many previous bets were lost.

The fascination with "best," "most celebrated," and "winner" also creates a society of losers which can increase Econ-Angst. Society's losers can even have a sense of fame in a perverse way, winning at losing. Losing can create celebrated losers: the 1962 Mets, ESPN's Hall of Flameouts, Greg Norman's 1996 Masters Tournament, and Sonny Liston's 1965 defeat by Muhammad Ali's "Phantom Punch." Steely Dan's 1976 lyrics champion the loser's plight with the lyrics of *Deacon Blues*,

"I want a name when I lose.

They call Alabama the Crimson Tide.

Call me Deacon Blues . . . Deacon Blues!"

Explaining this part of American Exceptionalism is not to be critical, but it is necessary to make a clear distinction with economic competition. Economic competition is defined in a special way. American culture's familiar sense of competition is foreign to economics. Economic competition recognizes consumers' and sellers' self-interests competing in a marketplace. At an agreed-upon market price, all players are winners. Sellers are satisfied with the profit from the supply quantity sold. Consumers achieve their satisfaction with the demand quantity bought. Sellers are winners because they are selling all the products they want to sell at the market's equilibrium price. The consumers are winners because they are buying all the products they want to buy at that same price.

Economists' concept of the "market" is where prices are discovered through demand and supply forces. On the supply side, firms want to be as efficient as possible to compete with others. On the demand side, consumers want to be efficient buyers to stretch their budget dollars. Supply and demand competitions create efficiency. *Businesses compete for customers* through pricing, special services, coupons, availability, and quality. *Consumers compete for available purchases with each other.* Once a product is bought, it becomes non-replaceable to another customer. For example, a building lot, once bought at an auction, cannot be purchased by another bidder. Consumers usually do not notice this competition until they sense a shortage, and then they realize that once the last product is bought, they can no longer buy it. Think of the rush to buy the most popular holiday toy.

This market concept is the economists' model of perfect economic competition. It is held as the most efficient way to use resources as production inputs. When a market's price makes the sellers' quantity equal to the buyers' quantity, there is no waste. Sellers will be content to provide the quantity that buyers want to purchase at the agreed-upon price. There is no product scarcity and no product surplus in the market. If there are, market prices will adjust—increasing with scarcity and decreasing with surplus.

Firms target least-cost production to be able to sell in price- competitive markets. However, there is a difference between businesses' accounting costs and economic costs. The economic cost is the accounting cost *plus* the industry's normal profit to ownership. This normal profit is the economic return to owners' (entrepreneurs') for risk and work. It is the cost of the owner. The competitive model guards against owners' greed by holding prices down. The model assumes that there would be other firms in the market so that no firm would have the power to raise their prices for additional profit. If a firm tried, the market would punish it because the other firms would undercut the higher price. The advantage of a free market is to reduce government regulation and interference.

Economists not only hold perfect competition as a measure of efficiency but also as a guide to regulate certain non-competitive markets. They realize that perfect competition does not usually exist in the economy, but it is useful for regulatory government agencies and panels in concentrated markets. Such agencies make rulings and recommendations for local utilities, bridges, tunnels, and toll road fees, and enforce competition in monopoly-type industries. Cairn 3 develops an understanding of economic competition as a necessary component of the economy. The competitive model of perfect competition satisfies the need for market efficiency and promotes supply and demand winners.

There is another way in which economists differ from business accountants. It is how costs are viewed. Business costs are for inputs and fixed overhead used in production. But missing are the negative external costs to the environment and society. The new economic citizen needs to be aware of these additional economic costs of social well-being and environmental resources. Industrial costs may not include costs of noise pollution, human illnesses, air pollution, water contamination, nuclear contamination, or chemical poisoning. These external costs must be corrected and paid for. Market competition does not accurately measure the costs in these industries. The question of who pays for the external costs has sparked debate. Proposals have been suggested for private sector remedies and for federal government payments to cover remedial costs through taxation. Determining who pays is crucial to the economic concept of market costs and competition, but in any case, they must be lessened or eliminated. Capitalism's dependence upon a free-market economy rests with the resolution of the public/private debate over negative externality costs to society and the environment.

Standard economic competition is taught in economics classes across the world. To a business, the result of inefficiency is a loss of profit, market share, or loss of competitiveness. To an economist, waste and inefficiency are costs to the economy equal to the loss of resources. When waste is characteristic of an economy, it becomes a danger to its citizens and its existence. Earth's sustainability for human existence demands a second look at free market competition.

The perfectly competitive model only sees production resources as input costs that are calculated into a firm's supply prices. However, companies may not see environmental cleanup as input costs. Firms have traditionally not included the cost of negative externalities. The damage to the planet's resources (negative external costs) is not calculated into a company's costs to produce cement tonnage or combustion engine autos. One firm may end up paying more for short-supply inputs (scarcer resources). But the company's production plans commit a type of *fallacy of composition (what is true of one is true of all)*. A fallacy occurs, here, when one firm says it can afford to pay more for a scarce resource input. One company can afford it, but all companies cannot afford it *because the earth cannot afford it*; hence the illogic, *what is true of one is not true for all.*

Considering a demand-and-supply market efficiency is necessary, but not sufficient, to slow damage to the earth's systems and resources. Even if the train is running efficiently, we must not run it off the cliff. When the earth's resource sustainability is considered, an extension of market competition must be made which here is called "*economic competition+.*" It includes market competition *plus* the competition to maintain and save earth's sustainability. Understanding the competition for sustainability is an *additional requirement of economic citizenship for individuals, governments, and businesses.*

ECONOMIC COMPETITION+

Fortune magazine enhanced its Change the World List of companies for 2023. The additionally listed companies were those better at developing innovative ways to reach pollution-net-zero and sustain earth's resources. The list also highlighted those having better ways for workers to adapt skills to technological change and better ways to tackle global challenges to food and health care availability.

There already exist effective tools to help save the earth's resources, including programs of anti-dumping, recycling, repurposing, cleaning the oceans and air, advancing clean energy, retooling utilities for green energy, constructing green buildings, and renewing efficiency of the older construction. Economic activity must be measured against economic competition+. Shareholders of corporations and citizens of communities need to be re-educated. Profits are not enough to justify capitalism's success. *Economics' moral imperative demands the incentive of profit to include resource sustainability for national wealth and citizens' well-being.*

Economic competition+ holds company management and shareholders to a moral and existential imperative of earth's sustainability. Sustainability awareness and progress for public and corporate mobilization have had some progress.

- *Awareness* of sustainability is displayed in New York City's 62-foot-long Climate Clock, which references the 2015 Paris Climate Accords that set benchmarks to halt the impending 2030 climate crisis. This international treaty's goal is to diminish the earth's warming that contributes to increases of catastrophic heatwaves, wildfires, storms, and sea levels.

- *Public participation* in local recycling programs and waste separation ordinances has had some success. The US Environmental Protection Agency reported in 2022 that the national recycling rate went from about 7% in 1960 to about 32%. But the effectiveness of plastic recycling has been questioned by organizations such as Greenpeace, the 5 Gyres Institute, and on National Public Radio programming (October 24, 2022). The plastic wastage is present in floating isles in areas of the seas. The Great Pacific Garbage Patch has 80,000 tons of plastic garbage located between California and the Hawaiian Islands.

- *Corporate adoption and participation* in sustainability measuring is monitored by The Ceres organization, which has issued reports since 2014. They showed that, even though corporations have been slow to take responsibility, there has been improvement in top management's sustainability leadership in production and supply chains.
- *Scorecard* (2021) rated the major greenhouse gas emitting countries' commitment and their activities to achieve emission targets by 2030 and 2050. The United States fell into the "some progress" category of the twenty-five-country's rating: only ahead of

Russia, India, Mexico, Nigeria, China, Thailand, South Africa, Indonesia, Iran, India, Saudi Arabia, and Turkey.

- *The Environment, Social, and Governance I Report (ESG) Group rates companies' investment* opportunities according to their ESG factors. One rating factor is a company's green environmental approach to making a positive impact on the world around them. This incorporates the economic competition+ concept for investment opportunities.

The target year of 2030 is prescient and may foreshadow a climate point of no return for the earth's health. *Scorecard's* climate assessment is useful for world governments. Pressure is applied to nations that are environmental villains. Participating in economic competition+ is important for citizens' economic citizenship. What actions do they take daily to save the planet? Do they buy and use products that are harmful to the environment? What companies in their budget or investment portfolio are polluters? Do they work for a non-competitive+ company? They can vote with dollar expenditures. They can also vote at the ballot box for candidates who are green-friendly and will participate in governmental actions to address the earth's sustainability.

Historical context will help to understand the challenge that economic competition+ has when moving American capitalism more toward the economics' moral concern of the earth's sustainability. Sustainability must be seen across time because correcting the economy will take time. The proverbial ocean liner does not turn at a buoy marker.

The United States was assembled on a continent of enormous natural resources. The country constructed a favorable economic environment for companies that fostered private markets characterized by economic regulations, contract law, patent protections, corporate legal designation as "person," and anti-trust legislation. But the

American (and world) economy is not perfectly competitive. Over two-plus centuries, people of wealth gained economic power over market pricing and distribution. They were trying to gain monopoly power by maneuvering conditions to diminish economic competition.

American capitalism's story tells of times of monopoly formation and times of governmental anti-monopoly regulation. In the late 19th Century, monopolies appeared with the rise of the so-called "Robber Barons," who used clever and ruthless methods to eliminate the competition of smaller firms. Such men as Gould, Rockefeller, Carnegie, Morgan, Vanderbilt, and Duke built empires in railroads, oil, steel, finance, banking, transportation, and tobacco, respectively. Starting with the Sherman Anti-Trust Act of 1890, the federal government stepped in to enforce competition in these industries; however, the public energy for 20th Century anti-trust enforcement waned. Given the growth of corporate power, it seemed impractical to indict most of the economy. Mergers and buy-outs have eliminated competition even further for many industries. Twenty-first Century antitrust activity is still active in healthcare, aerospace, and construction industries, as well as with Monsanto, Amazon, Google, Facebook, and Microsoft.

This is not to say that there is not competition in the economy, just that business competition and wealth-winning competition tended to supplant democratic economic competition. Adam Smith's self-interest evolved into Wall Street greed[6], and economic competition morphed into collusion and the race for market power. Smith's notion of morality as an inhibitor of wealth accumulation was diluted by the commercialization of American society. The private interest overcame the public interest. Today, Americans drive expensive modern automobiles over poorly cared-for public roads, and beautifully designed sports complexes amass profits next to underserved residential communities.

Economists call the two major types of existing competition today monopolistic competition and oligopoly. Monopolistic competition occurs between small and medium-sized firms in the same regional market. They try to differentiate their products or services. If they are successful, and consumers or clients prefer only their product or service, they can operate as a monopolistic or mini monopoly. This type of competition occurs in fast food and pizza restaurants, branded clothing, and beauty salons. The firms in these sectors of the economy have similarities, but specialized services or product features make one appear different from another.

The second type of competition occurs with oligopolies, where there are only a few large firms that are in the same national or world market. Each one is in competition to carve out as much market share as possible. But they don't use price competition. They find price collusion and market-sharing cooperation as a better strategy to optimize profits. When an industry's top five firms control 60% of the market share, they can be considered oligopolies.

Oligopolies are found in the petroleum, airlines, mass media, and automobile industries. They have a national and international presence.

The desire for market power entices firms to use mergers or acquisitions for larger market power. Some examples of these combinations are Verizon and Vodafone, Heinz and Kraft, Pfizer and Warner-Lambert, AT&T and Time Warner, Exxon and Mobile, Google and Android, and Disney/Pixar and Marvel.

A large company with little economic competition is called a monopoly when it owns more than 70% of its market. This is far from the efficiency of the perfect competition. Monopoly and oligopoly profits accrue to shareholders and salaries of top management. Their bloated profits and salaries create national income and wealth inequalities. These companies can charge higher prices, so consumers pay more for what they purchase and buy less than they would otherwise. The country's railways, Google, Facebook, Luxottica (sunglasses), and Microsoft are considered monopolies. The United States government has the legal authority and responsibility to monitor monopoly profits and enforce benefits of the missing economic competition.

There is a debate regarding the benefits and detriments of capitalism's monopolies and oligopolies. The detriment side has been explained, but there is another side to the structure of America's economy. On the benefits side, monopolies and oligopolies possess long-run efficiencies of high-volume production's decreasing unit costs. It is unreasonable for new firms to enter into their markets because of high startup and fixed-cost barriers. Another barrier is the product and process protections afforded by U.S. patents (20 years), trademarks, and copyrights. Each year, about 350,000 United States patents are issued to enterprising businesses and individuals. The larger firms have the capacity to have Research and Development (R&D) Departments that use the protections to improve production, install technological efficiency, and advance the economy's growth. They must stay competitive in the industries that have aggressive pro-green and start-up companies. Capitalism's advantages of long-run cost and research efficiencies somewhat balance the disadvantages of their market power inefficiencies and income inequality.

America's concentration of economic power must address environmental sustainability and social well-being. This creates a new vision of the economic problem of scarcity. This century's scarcity is not defined *just* by increases of supply's input prices and quantities. It refers to the scarcity of the earth's natural resources. It includes all earth's living and non-living resources for human life, from industrial minerals and fertile ground to climate, clean water, and healthy air.

There have been warnings about environmental degradation for five-plus decades[7]. America and other world nations are in *existential competition* to sustain the planet and human life. We all will either be losers or winners. America's global-reach capitalism must now adopt economic competition+. It demands behavioral changes for the players in the economy. Citizen behavior, manufacturing industries, energy production, and governmental policies must conduct a revolution in a closing window of opportunity. The competitive+ objective must add environmental allocative efficiency to market efficiency. Capitalism's competitive players must include mission statements (words) and production plans (actions) to save our inhabitable and healthful environment. *Competition+ includes the economy's competition for sustainability.*

American capitalism must also address the new version of economic wealth. There is competition for society's well-being, and an economic argument that must be made for the sake of the social good. More than two centuries ago, Adam Smith made the point that a country's wealth is its productive capacity and not the storing of precious metals in the national treasury. Today, the same point needs making. Economic wealth is the productive capacity of the country and not the amassed accounts of billions of dollars in a few private financial accounts. It is increased by building bridges, not walls; by rewarding, not punishing; by educating, not indoctrinating; by appealing to reason, not to emotion; by conversing, not arguing; by being responsibly present, not absent; by sharing, not hoarding; and by being constructive, not disengaging. The business of capitalism requires the honesty and trust of citizens, companies, and government. Governmental participation in the economy must come from the authority of democratic participation. Advertising and marketing must contribute by appealing to society's well-being. The power of advertising must be used to trumpet the values of cooperation, anti-violence, intergroup cohesion, and the building of a safe community square. Messaging must deliver, in substance and in tone, diversity and inclusion as the norm of society. Forms of social entertainment need to explore themes of life's strategies of compromise. Economic c*ompetition+ includes the economy's competition for social well-being.*

The goal must be to redefine economic wealth accrued to the very few through business success—production efficiency and asset manipulation—to include preserving the earth's resources and promoting the public good.

Economic competition+ must be for economic activities that save, not waste, and renew, not dispose of. Businesses and nations that save and renew the earth's resources are the true competitors who will expand and flourish. Those who waste and dispose of will fail. Businesses and nations that develop and share civic values and economic rewards will expand and flourish. Those that destroy and hoard will fail. Those who love the earth must prevail.

Economic citizenship requires the adoption of economic competition+. Citizens must adjust to the "+" idea of being in competition with others to do their part as economic citizens of the country and earth. Consumer purchasing is a powerful force in a market. Companies monitor preferences, sales, and profits, and will bend to consumer choices. The goal of vast wealth accumulation and massive profits needs to take a back seat to the goals of improving the earth's health, society, and human well-being.

"Economic Wealth includes Earth Health."

"Economic Profit includes Human Health."

The United States is in the throes of a post-industrial era. Is increasing income and wealth still taking precedent over environment sustainability? Economic competition+ must be experienced at the personal, societal, and planetary levels. Because corporations dominate the American economy, it is imperative for their leaders to compete for the earth's sustainability.

Large firms with higher industry concentrations in the economy have contributed to increased productivity (efficiency) and economic growth. They have the power to make sustainability decisions. Their efforts for sustainability must be nurtured and rewarded by a newly competitive+ society. One such effort is the energy platform company, *Envision*, which has led economic competition+ by partnering with leading organizations to help achieve a world that has access to clean, secure, and affordable energy through renewable technology and smart management. Private sector companies have advanced economic competition+ by advertising the ideal of social responsibility. The federal government's Clean Energy Act (2009) as well as the Environmental Protection Agency (1970), and state environmental departments have demonstrated that some companies may not adhere to competition+ without government enforcement. Over the last fifty years, they have worked on their missions for cleaner air and waterways, but more actions are needed. The SET continues to increase. Efficiency has not kept pace with the 21st Century's scarcity.

INCOME AND WEALTH INEQUALITY

The American economy's income and wealth profile is problematic. Twenty-first Century corporations and shareholders derive passive income and asset wealth that has dwarfed the income from workers in the labor force. There are negative consequences to inequality. Unequal income distribution increases Econ-Angst for working citizens. Can you really get rich by working as an employee?

Citizens lose the motivation to work for success. There is a thin line in the race between giving up or continuing to strive. This motivational battle can be lost as far back as K-12 grade students. In an industrial school concept, grades are competitive. There are winners and losers. Losers stop competing for grades. At some point, they realize that they are behind and can never match the effort to be a successful learner. They feel that they are in a competition for grades that they can't win. We hear *"I can't do math!" or "I'll never be an artist!" or "I don't like my teacher!"* from exasperated students.

Is it the fault of the student or the schoolhouse? The answer breaks both ways. Students graduate on the wrong side of this thin line. In searching for solutions, the blame game is counterproductive. Citizens who fail serve up explanations and reasons. It is safe to say that lack of educational support and investment in America's human resources has resulted in an educational deficit. This may not be by accident because the result is increased inequality in America's distribution of wealth and income. In 2023, the top 10% of households owned about 29 times more *wealth* than the bottom 50%.[8] In 2021, the top 10% of households earned 13.53 times more *income* than the bottom 10%[9]. This maldistribution has left most of the population struggling for the resources necessary to enjoy the fruits of increased productivity. Econ-Angst is a reaction among losers amid poverty and powerlessness. Workers strive not necessarily for wealth as much as to have the opportunity to fully participate in the advantages of the economy.

Is this new? What do we see when looking at wealth distribution across historical civilizations? Great civilizations of Central America, South America, Babylonia, China, Africa, Central Asia, and Europe have risen and fallen with a top powerful class amassing wealth at the expense of the larger lower classes. Democratic governments of Europe and North America in recent history have attempted to break this pattern. Unequal income and wealth distribution are not goals of modern economics or of America's democratic government. From 1950 to 2000,

US corporate profits and labor wages followed the same growth trend, with the gap staying about the same. But beginning around the turn of the century, productivity increases have flowed to corporate profits and largely outpaced labor wages[10]. Capitalism's engine for growth has run into a problem: expanding income and wealth inequality,

According to the Congressional Budget Office CBO (2016)[11], the United States *income gap* before federal taxes and benefit transfers was as follows:

- *The average income among households in the lowest quintile—the lowest 20%--of the income distribution was about $21,000.*
- *The average income among households in the highest quintile was about $291,000, and*
- *The average income among households in the top 1% was about $1.8 million.*

After the application of taxes and benefit transfers, the income gap was lessened, but still showed a high level of inequality.

In 2023, an estimate by the Statistica Research Department[12] of the U.S. *wealth gap* looked like this:

- *The top 10% of households owned 69% of the nation's wealth,*
- *The bottom 50% own 2.4%.*

This picture of the economy is disturbing. Cairn 3 recognizes the challenge of the economy's inequality. Econ-Angst must not become indifferent or despair of it. Newer ideas must be implemented for better outcomes. There is an existential co-dependence of the top and bottom of the distribution created by the environmental crisis. The new battle ground for winning the new economic competition+ will need to champion well-being at the personal, societal, and planetary levels. It will involve some combination of increased labor leverage, progressive taxation, sharing external social costs, government enforcement of regulations, corporate conscience, and efficient use of new technologies. But most of all, *the responsibility for economic winning rests with each individual citizen adopting the new economic citizenship.* The default position of workers must not be to drop out of the labor force or depend on government aid programs. The default position of corporate wealth must not be to blame those in poverty. The default position of the planet must not be left to the degradation of resources, warming climate, and destruction of land, sea, and air ecologies. There must be a coordinated effort to correct the degradation of the planet's resources and to better distribute opportunities and support for income and wealth. The *new economic citizenship recognizes that everyone is in the same boat.*

CAIRN 4: RECOGNIZING OPPORTUNITY COSTS

"Economists point out that the quality value of any given option cannot be assessed in isolation from its alternatives. One of the costs of any option involves passing up

the opportunities that a different option would have afforded."

--Barry Schwartz

"The dream is free...but the journey will cost you something."

--John C. Maxwell

When making economic decisions, you look for choices that give you opportunity benefits; for example, moving to a different state for increased employment opportunities, or using networks of face-to-face or digital connections to help a business startup. You know that there will be costs associated with these decisions, but *opportunity costs* are not the familiar dollar costs that show up in invoices, ledgers, or budgets. Opportunity costs in economics are the costs of the second-best alternative, the lost value of benefits not taken. If resources are dedicated to one choice at the expense of the second, the opportunity cost is the value of the second choice. Once a choice is made to do or buy one thing, the resources to do or buy the other are lost. The economic cost borne by the first includes the opportunity loss of the second. Examples of opportunity costs are:

- *If a student decides to attend a university with a $30,000 tuition cost, the student also incurs the loss of a $24,000 job offer. This makes the economic cost of attending the university $54,000, the tuition plus the opportunity cost of the job.*
- *If a family is planning a vacation and is excited about going to the mountains or the islands. The opportunity cost for choosing the island vacation includes the value of the lost time and the happiness of the mountain vacation.*
- *If a company has a choice either to expand an existing product's production or to start a new product's production line, choosing one will incur the cost of the other. In choosing one, the opportunity benefit of the other is lost.*
- *If a country wants to either fix interstate roadways or maintain military bases in foreign countries,*

choosing one over the other incurs the opportunity cost of the other. Maintaining military bases also costs travel improvements, commuter travel time, and additional air pollution.

- *If a worker changes a $30,000-per-year job for one with a salary of $35,000 per year, the benefit to the worker is $5,000 after considering the opportunity cost.*

Calculating opportunity cost is a powerful factor. Expanding decision-making to include the economic costs of opportunity promotes a more realistic life picture of choices. When a family decides to buy a new car, the calculation must include what else the money might do for the family. When there is a scarcity of household money and resources, the effect of adding the opportunity cost is felt more. Decisions must be carefully calculated.

CAIRN 5: USING MARGINAL ANALYSIS

"The man who moves a mountain begins by carrying away small stones."

--Confucius

Economists use marginal analysis to assess the process and progress of actions and the values of items. One common example of marginal analysis is the choice about which is more valuable, diamonds or water. Given a chance to think about it, a person would conclude that water is necessary for life and, therefore, of more value. A human's value for water-in-total has much more value than a compressed hunk of coal. However, given the choice of a large-cut diamond or *a drink* of water most people would take the diamond. This makes sense because a drink of water is one of many taken. It is called *at the margin* of wanting water. Now, what if the situation were changed to a person who was suffering from extreme dehydration being given the same choice? The drink's marginal value would be greater than the diamond.

Confusing the difference between total and marginal leads to poor and inefficient choices. The marginal analysis of water drinking illustrates better decision-making. Taking the value of a diamond and one drink of water, the diamond usually wins, but at the margin for a dehydrated person, the drink of water is chosen. One can drink water repeatedly until there is no marginal value left, even though the total amount of water needed for life is existentially (in total) valued. Economists consider choices made at the margins as efficient.

The consideration of the margin is important for decision-making in business. A business will expand its production to maximize its profits up until the cost of making the next (marginal) product unit is equal to the sale revenue of that unit. Economists call this the *marginal cost-marginal revenue equality point (MC=MR).* Marginal costs, at some point of production, increase. They will increase because extra workers may be hired at a higher competitive wage, overtime wages may increase labor costs, or additional office or warehouse space may have to be rented. If expansion of production causes MC to be greater than MR, then total profits will decrease.

The consideration at the margin is important for consumers as well; for example, when purchasing pairs of shoes, there is a point where the cost of the next pair is greater than the marginal benefit to the consumer. By using marginal analysis, the decision is made to stop buying pairs of shoes even though the consumer may still like them. Retailers understand this marginal calculation. They run discounts (BOGOs, three for the price of two, buy one get the second at 50%) on the additional product items to match the consumer's lower marginal benefits. For maximum profit, each purchase or sale is calculated as *one transaction or lot or run at a time*. For maximum consumer benefit, each item purchased is calculated as one item per transaction.

The economic citizen will usually learn this through repeated ill-advised actions in the role of consumer or businessperson. Cairn 5 will stop you from overbuying products or services in bulk before finding out the lower marginal benefits of the additional items. Did you end up with a case of Peanut Butter with one jar of Jelly? *Take one step, assess the situation, evaluate, decide, and take one step again.*

CAIRN 6: LIVING BY A NEW WORK ETHIC

". . . try and get up every morning, day after day and work for a livin'! . . . Then we'll see who's the REAL tough guy! The working man's the tough guy! Your father's the tough guy!"

--Lorenzo Anello to his son, Calogero, in A Bronx Tale

The America Dream is a well-worn idea in American culture. It has been the dominant dream during the country's history but was not coined as such until 1931 when the term, American Dream, was popularized by James Truslow Adams' book, *Epic of America*[13]. It celebrated the ideal of freedom for citizens to prosper. It held the hope (promise?) of opportunities for success through adherence to hard work and sacrifice. The idea has been carried by centuries of immigrants up to this day.

Immigrants with American Dreams have not always been welcome. The dream of economic opportunity was not immediately realized. Immigration laws and quotas were not always friendly to populations of diverse religions, ethnicity, race, or social standing. Most of today's American population had ancestors who fought for their dreams. The door was closed at times except for the African slaves who came as property. But it remains the dream for many that *the United States is still a land of opportunity.*

Americans were also holding a similar dream-idea. It was called the *Protestant Ethic.*[14] Besides the rewards of the work ethic, it promised the reward of *eternal salvation* for the worldly success. These two ideas of the land of opportunity and work's salvation have held cultural prominence. But they have not been alone; there has been a counter-dream.

Another American dreamscape was explored by authors Kurt Anderson, and Ben McKenzie and Jacob Silverman.[15] It involves what is called *fantasyland*—the whatever-you-want culture of make-believe. It is an extension of private investment casino capitalism, where players take risks for a big payoff. It becomes *fascination capitalism* where consumers seek and find emotional payoffs from dreams, magic, and hucksters. It plays to continuous gambling, vacuous buying, wow-entertainment, elation habits, thrill-seeking, cultural fetishes, and ultra-individualism. It, too, is as American as apple pie. In fascination capitalism, playing the odds of the game replaces the daily grind, luck and chance replace hard work, and planned economic goals melt under the heat of possibly winning and the belief in the fantastic. This has happened to the American culture even though economic success has proven not to be a singular event. Illusions overlay reality. Impulsivity and emotions bury calculation and reason. Money becomes the symbol of well-being and happiness. A winner can be crowned at the carnival's wheel of fortune.

Winning money and what it can buy is the quick fix of lotteries, consumer chance opportunities, betting, gambling, and investment schemes. It is difficult to estimate personal expenditures on gaming, betting, and ad-driven consumer purchases, but it is omnipresent. The Federal Reserve of St. Louis estimated the consumer expenditures on legal betting in the US topped $160B in 2022;[16] while legal *sports* betting alone in 2023 is estimated to be $250B.[17]

The *fantasy economy* can become a lifestyle for consumers of wishes, luck, and chance. The opportunity cost of fantasy is time and energy taken from work, but citizens will pay that cost for engaging in illusions. Gambling and playing chances may have a place in a household's entertainment budget, but the problem occurs when gambling goes beyond entertainment. The National Council on Problem Gambling estimates the yearly costs of problem gambling in the United States to be $7 Billion. This includes criminal justice, healthcare spending, job loss, and bankruptcy. The Council also sees the yearly consequences *directly* affecting up to six million people.

Unfortunately, gaming may act as a strategy in the real economic world of working, saving, paying bills, or investing. It ends up being a losing play. Gaming has a high opportunity cost and can lead to gambling addiction, personal dishonesty, and illegal activities.

Cairn 6 is the reminder of c*ourage to believe in yourself, your talents, your strengths, and your goals*. Success in life involves meeting the responsibilities of life and work. Working on your strategic plan for job and career enhancement is the path of the American Dream. The work ethic, however, can be eroded by unnecessary risk-taking and chance-playing, so it is up to the individual to stay on the economic course of well-thought-out decisions. Living in an impoverished situation or with an impoverished attitude may cry out for a quick solution, but there is no "easy way." Following the dream of a "winner's chance" is a slippery slope to economic losses. Keep the work ethic at the fore.

Cairn 6 borrows from the first two dreams centered on the value of work and well-planned strategies for success. It is the way to lessen Econ-Angst and is the way of the responsible economic citizen. The fantasy economy's hook reads, "You can't win it . . . if you're not in it." Cairn 6 answers with, "You can't lose . . . if you're not in it."

Jimmy Buffett put the work ethic poetically in the 1981 song, *It's My Job*:

In the middle of late last night, I was sittin' on a curb.
I didn't know what about, but I was feelin' quite disturbed.
A street sweeper came whistlin' by, he was bouncin'
every step. It seemed strange how good he felt, so I asked

him while he swept. He said,
"It's my job to be cleaning
up this mess, and that's enough reason to go for me.
It's my job to be better than the rest,
and that makes a day for me."

A last note about union membership: let your eco-self look at the world of work from 30,000 feet. Work should be understood in the larger picture of the workforce that makes up about 63% of the population. The employee/employer relationship has been shaped over the years by labor unions that have protected employee rights and benefits. Their power has diminished in the last decades. The story of union status in the American workforce shows that union representation has been inconsistent. It began in the late 19th Century. In the mid-20th Century, it increased membership under judicial and legal protection. In the late 20th and early 21st Century, membership decreased. In 1983, it stood at 20.1% of the labor force; in 2015, it stood at 11.3% (6% in the private sector)[18] and has remained constant since.

The effect of lower union participation is largely felt at the bargaining table for wages and work environment. Leverage is usually tilted toward ownership. Southern states have lower union membership than the national averages. This decrease has been associated with stagnant real wages in the face of inflation over the last 40 years. Four factors have disempowering labor. First, Right to Work laws were adopted in 28 states. They weakened union membership while expanding workers' economic freedom. Second, employer-sponsored 401(k) retirement plans have been substituted for union pensions with the effect of moving retirement risk and shifting control of investment decisions from professional investors to employees. Third, companies have fought union membership to lower costs. And fourth, union membership has not kept pace with the newer tech and communication industries.

CAIRN 7: INVESTING IN YOURSELF

"The most valuable of all capital is that invested in human beings."

--Alfred Marshall

"Your present circumstances don't determine where you can go; they merely determine where you start."

--Nido Qubein

Economists view citizens as members of the labor force and as one of the factors in economic growth—physical capital, natural resources, technology, entrepreneurship, and human resources. Economists see citizens as human resources and national assets. One major difference between a post-industrial country and an emerging-economy country is the quality of human resources, including workers' values, attitudes, skills, and knowledge. Important drivers of capitalism are inventiveness, motivation, and management skills, all nurtured by opportunities and education. *New economic citizenship sees the need for continuous knowledge and skill training both for the interest of the worker and as an advantage to the economy.*

America's 20th Century compulsory K-12 public education requirements and optional post-high school education were instituted to meet the needs of an industrial economy. Today, this educational structure is not sufficient for an economy dominated by services, technology, and knowledge and conceptual management. State governments still do not require schooling past twelfth grade. There is an economic debate about whether governments should pay for post-high school education. Some states have created methods for paying parts of the post-high school, but the nation is still adjusting its educational menu to benefit post-industrial employment needs. A debate carries over regarding the benefit of year-round public-school schedules.

Cairn 7 shows the importance of educational investments in yourself but also for the country's economy. Paying school taxes, tuition, and fees are the costs of investing in individuals' knowledge level and skill sets. It is also a way of enriching the country's human resources to meet the demands of a modern economy.

Let us examine the investment payout. A common question of students is in what asset should they invest. My reply is always, "yourself," because that investment has advantages for eco-self and your lifetime payout (future earned income and wealth). So, what does the educational investment payout look like?

The United States Bureau of Labor Statistics finds a positive relationship between the level of education and the level of weekly income for workers aged twenty-five and over. For the year 2021, those with less than a high school diploma earned an average weekly wage of $626. Average weekly income rose with increased higher educational investment: high school diploma ($809); some college, no degree ($899); associate's degree ($963); bachelor's degree ($1334); master's degree ($1574); and over

$1900 weekly for those with professional or doctoral degrees.[19] Initially, there is the opportunity cost of an entry-level job; however, many students also hold such a job to pay for their education.

Income lost through unemployment can damage education's payout and interfere with career plans. The pattern indicates lower unemployment rates for those with higher education. Unemployment rates for 2021 found the lowest educational level had the highest unemployment rate, while the highest educational levels had the lowest rate.[20]

A 2021 yearly investment payout for education is below:

Median Salary by Education Level

Education Level	**Male**	**Female**	**National Median Annual Wage**
Less than 9th grade	$29,334	$17,876	$24,965
Some high school	$29,775	$18,824	$24,988
High school completion	$39,953	$27,000	$33,996
Some college, no degree	$47,587	$31,146	$38,919
Associate degree	$51,999	$34,994	$41,986
Bachelor degree	$69,983	$50,000	$59,913
Master's degree	$89,812	$62,488	$70,941
Doctoral degree	$119,899	$84,453	$100,000
Professional degree	$124,580	$92,347	$102,265

Source: National Center for Education Statistics, 2021

Both weekly and yearly earning measurements yielded the same relationship, reinforcing the saying, "Education doesn't cost, it pays." It pays for both men and women. Women, however, have consistently been paid less in the same work category as men. According to the U.S. Census Quarterly Workforce Indicators (2020, 3rd quarter), U.S. women earned 30% less than men.

The educational level-income relationship remains across the arc of *workers' lifetime* earning years.[21] The lifetime income arc shows average yearly earnings increasing for workers in their early 20s, peaking between ages 45 to 54, and decreasing after the age of 65. But those with higher education degrees can show average lifetime earnings that are millions of dollars greater than those at the high school level. Men's earnings again are higher than women's, but both have a significant differential between higher education and high school.

These trends are based on national categories and averages. It is cautionary, however, to note that there are differences in various states and regions of the country, and in specific job categories. National statistics can cover up data pockets.

The need for further educational investment can cost time and opportunity. But by following Cairn 7 and making educational investment decisions, you can ease Econ-Angst. Planning for educational investment can be spread over time through budgeting. The result of educational saving will garner motivation, uplift eco-self, increase focus, and gain information about labor needs and educational institutions' offerings. Twenty-first Century careers do not necessarily coincide with traditional trade skills or with higher-ed majors from the last century. If you have an analog brain, digital training is needed for current-century skills. Initial educational advancement or repositioning careers may be accomplished through part-time attendance or a brief work hiatus.

University attendance ages 18-24 in 2022 was about 38%.[22] Students were seeking more professional, business, or scientific careers. Preparing for in-demand interdisciplinary careers can be accomplished by double-majoring or enrolling in interdisciplinary studies. Delaying the declaration of a college major while in college can enrich the knowledge of liberal arts and science fields. This may expand choices for those continuing to search for a career that fits passion, interest, and salary.

Post-high school technology institutions are also available to match future work placement. Community colleges (22% of high school graduates[23]) provide career-ready and technical job programs. High schools across the nation have Career and Technical Education (CTE) paths that enroll students in internships, jobs, or further training in technical schools. Both community colleges and CTE opportunities have emerged as a growing and lower-cost source for advanced technical and career training.

In any case, before decision time, "Do your homework!." *Each year millions of highly skilled jobs go unfilled because of a lack of qualified applicants.* Employment opportunities at future's edge are fertile ground for a worker of any age.

So far, Cairn 7 has examined the effect of formal education on income, but informal education plays an important part as well. It occurs when workers cooperate, converse, demonstrate, and pass experiential knowledge and skills amongst themselves. It is referred to as on-the-job training. For generations, career and job information has been passed on to families and neighborhoods. Formal schooling may not be sufficient for employment success when actual on-the-job experience, attitudes, skills, and knowledge are needed as the "teacher."

An enormous amount of informal education lies outside of the lessons of school. There are many opportunities to educate yourself through videos, topical reading, textbooks, or discussions with peers. Google searches, Wikipedia, library offerings, and YouTube's informational selections provide ample sources to satisfy curiosity and fill in informational gaps. But in the end, earning as many certificates, licenses, memberships, awards, letters of commendation, and degrees as possible is the marketable currency for establishing employment. *Americans have been accused of entertaining themselves to death. Cairn 7 represents the alternative: educating ourselves for life.*

Unemployment can suppress yearly earnings and can be the result of cyclical (recessionary) downturns or restructuring of industries. Both causes are imposed upon workers and are outside of their control; however, they can be mitigated with Cairn 7's emphasis on educational investment. Technical schools and community colleges fill seats during recessions. The new century demands constant retraining and educational renewal to keep up with economic changes and employment opportunities. *The educational investment strategy must be lifelong learning.* It must include *being good at learning how to learn. Lifelong earning depends on lifelong learning*, whether it is of a formal or informal kind. An initial infusion of education for job and career paths is necessary but not sufficient. Sufficiency requires dedication to constant economic education. The question of "What am I going to be?" has been replaced by "How am I going to continue to be successfully employed?"

The dynamic nature of America's economy has the danger of leaving adult workers behind. Facing the possibility of unemployment or underemployment is a serious stressor, and the danger can be sudden or occur earlier than one expects. Previous knowledge and specific career skills have shorter shelf lives. Cairn 7 eases the distress. An additional educational investment makes it possible to improve your outlook, bolster your eco-self, lessen the danger of being left out of the labor force, dodge being partially employed, or being employed at a lower wage.

Forward-looking companies addressing this danger may offer in-house training, on-going professional requirements, apprenticeships, internships, or educational reimbursement for workers. Taking advantage of these types of re-educations will make the path to success less stressful. Without in-house opportunities, workers will incur additional educational costs. Community colleges, night classes, university graduate programs, unemployment retraining programs, and technical schools welcome back adults who are changing employment, re-entering the labor market, or re-educating and adjusting their employment skills and knowledge. These attendees have a wide range of ages.

Cairn 7 explains the necessity and nature of educational investment:

- *It changes compulsory education into continuous education,*
- *It re-writes the conversation from, "I can't afford to go back to school," to "I can't afford not to go back to school,"*
- *It changes life's goal of one job or career to the next job or career, and by realizing that:*
- *For much of the last century, it was enough for many to have a high school diploma with on-the-job training to have a factory job that would place a worker in the middle class, but*
- *In the new century, just a high school diploma alone will not gain entrance into the middle class,*

- *In last century, formal education was primarily seen only for children and youth, but*
- *In the new century, a combination of formal, informal, and continuous adult education will be necessary for membership in the middle class.*

Cairn 7 shreds these stubborn last-century views. They are as useless as a push lawn mower or a rotary phone. They will only increase frustrations and anxieties, making the economic journey harder.

"Do what you can, with what you've got, where you are."

--Theodore Roosevelt.

CAIRN 8: BRANDING YOURSELF

"All of us need to understand the importance of branding. We are CEOs of our own companies: Me Inc. To be in business today, our most important job is to be head marketer for the brand called You." -- Tom Peters, Fast Company, "The Brand Called You."

"The 5 Cs of personal branding are: Clarity, Cohesive, Consistent, Content, and Community."
--Robyn Graham, Linkedin (April 2019)

In the 2010's decade, articles were written about a burgeoning new job category. One that was not a traditional employee of a corporation or firm, but rather one that had a short-term project connection, and then was gone. Hundreds of thousands of information technology and digital experts took residence around the world, not really thinking of themselves as immigrants or citizens of a country. The job category took unofficial names such as "worker tourist," "technomad," or "digital nomad[24]." These members of a digital Wi-Fi community were not interested in having corporations control their status as employees. They were promoting themselves as a branded unique talent.

The long history of promoting eco-self in a workspace began with the early medical doctors, dentists, and lawyers. They were professionals who made a name for themselves and hung a shingle outside their offices. The same idea was furthered by singers, musicians, entertainers, and media personalities, authors, journalists, and sports figures who have carved out, and cashed in on, an image that appeals to consumers. Social media sites and podcasts have expanded and furthered these personal brandings in the economy.

In years past, record companies, movies, TV studios, and sports ownerships would have stables of performers under an exclusive employment contract. Early musical performers were under the control of record or agent contracts with little ability to take control of their image or own their musical product. A breakthrough occurred in the 1960s with a record deal between Ray Charles and ABC Paramount. Ray Charles gained ownership of the master tapes of his musical output. Today, most major artists own their masters. Many start their record labels: Jay-Z, Prince, Madonna, The Beatles, Diddy, Eminem, Katy Perry, and Kanye West just to name a few. Social media outlets and cottage-industry quality recordings and videos have given exposure to talents in music that otherwise would not be available. The music industry constantly demands new talent for new demographics and younger listeners. These newly branded performers fill the void.

The movie industry in the 1930s controlled the production and distribution of movies. The control included actor employment. The employee contracts were written by the major movie studios, such as MGM, RKO Pictures, and 20th Century Fox, to control actors' movie roles, public images, and their overall conduct. It wasn't until 1948, in an anti-trust Supreme Court case, that the studios lost the leverage of control. Today, actors are not signed to studios but sign acting contracts on a movie-by-movie basis. Their brand is more important than the motion picture company.

Up until Curt Flood's Supreme Court 1972 case involving free agency, Major League Baseball had strict employee rules over player careers and salaries. More cases and the rise of the Major League Players Association have given players more leverage over their images, work conditions, choice of teams, and salaries. Top stars in professional sports can determine not only their own brand but also choose their teams.

Collegiate athletes recently won a deal for the right to control their Name, Image, and Likeness (NIL) when university sports use their images in promotions. College athletes can also profit from product sponsorship and paid promotions. This gives them monetary incentives for where and under what conditions to perform. Young men and women gained additional leverage to create a brand for collegial enrollment that was unavailable to them a few years ago.

These situations and personalities have shown the way for employees to develop a talent that can be branded for a more modern relationship with businesses and corporations. Businesses large and small have shed ancillary services and operations by subcontracting and outsourcing specific areas of production. Their aim was to reduce in-house costs and relieve management of inefficient tasks. This development has opened the doors for niche companies and unique products or process businesses.

International outsourcing can be overcome with the proper application of technologies and digital communication firms within the United States. An inventor can become a branded business; a talented worker can become a branded business; and a clever once-employee can become a branded business. Many small businesses have morphed from sole proprietorships and partnerships to Limited Liability Corporations (LLC's). LLCs increased since the Internal Revenue Service provided its tax category in 1993.

The COVID-19 pandemic opened the door for more remote work arrangements between employers and employees. In cases where "homeworking" is beneficial for both, it is a small step to change employee links into branded subcontractors. This adjustment can make it a win-win.

Cairn 8 focuses on expanding the nature and opportunities of branded abilities. Not everyone can hit a 97-mph fastball or sing like Taylor Swift, but everyone can discover something to feature in their workspaces. The goal is to find a talent or interest that matches a distinct area of a firm's operations, promote the opportunity and its value, and attempt to rework the relationship with the employer. It will improve your attitude and, maybe, even your salary.

Small business products or services are a major outlet for branding. Digital designs, website' icons and logos, and competitive naming are the new century's manner of hanging out a shingle. According to the U.S. Small Business Administration (2023), there are 33.2 million small businesses, accounting for 44% of economic activity, and making up 99.9% of all businesses in the United States. Some are "brick," some are "click," and some are "brick-&-click." Your ability and attitude will determine your desired brand. The independence of working for yourself entices millions in the economy.

In an industry that does not fit the independent nature of branding, there are opportunities for an employee to shine as a team or shift member. Your eco-self must promote your worth as a unique employee or businessperson. Branding handles can emerge in a workspace such as "the idea gal," "the go-to employee," or "employee of the month." These can add value to employee contracts, bonus categories, or employee status perks.

Formal and informal branding has a unique workspace in the new economy. It takes the out-of-control anxiety of an employee and makes it a growth experience that takes advantage of opportunities as a business owner, independent contractor, subcontractor, or designated special employee. It is far from the mindset of a "worker bee," "forgotten drone," "shoulder-to-the-wheel," or "nose-to-the-grindstone" employee. It is not suck-up self-promotion. It is seizing opportunities that can polish your eco-self and ease Econ-Angst.

CAIRN 9: REALIZING CHANGE IS THE ONLY CONSTANT

"We can pretend that extending the status quo into the future, unchanged, is one of the options available to us. But that is a fantasy. Change is coming one way or another. Our choice is whether we try to shape that change to the maximum benefit of all or wait passively as the

forces of climate disaster, scarcity, and fear of the 'other' fundamentally reshape us."

-- Naomi Klein.

"We are living through the most profound changes in the economy since the Industrial Revolution. Technology, globalization, and the accelerating pace of change have yielded chaotic markets, fierce competition, and unpredictable staff requirements."

--Bruce Tulgan

The capacity of humans to adopt new ways of thinking and behaving is a challenge of this century's third decade. Workers may stay in the routine of a 20th Century job or career that was mastered years ago, but the shelf life of those skills is fading fast. The problem for many is the difficulty of getting comfortable with the skills of tomorrow's economy, especially when tomorrow's sunrise is occurring today. *The economic tomorrow is this morning.*

The introduction of new technologies starts in the economy because that is where it is profitable. These technologies will overrun your age group's work tools, skills, schedules, attitudes, and behaviors. It does not matter in what work-age decade you were educated. The change will bite you. Your strategic response is your defense.

Cultural norms and traditions are discarded as rapidly as new ones are created. Whole fields and careers are renovated seemingly overnight. Innovations in medicine, astronomy, communications (5G), data storage (off-site Cloud), manufacturing, transportation, GPS systems, Artificial Intelligence, and war-making are trumpeted around the world by 24-hour news programming and social media platforms. Smart cars, homes, and buildings are available. "Learning Culture" has become the mantra for the culture's demand for constant training and education. Didn't we just change the email protocols? Running is necessary to keep pace. High or medium-level digital skills are necessary for most jobs and careers.

The pace of change is part of the challenge, but awareness of another part is needed. It is managing and responding to changes that are equitable, inclusive, and planet sustainable. What are the changes' effects on minority groups, gender identification, and cultural cohesion? Does the pace of change promote the public good or improve the population's health? What harm is being done to the environment by economic growth and new technologies?

Looking at the economic landscape, we find that big box stores, professional sales services, and shopping malls (*brick* shopping sites) are giving way to *Click* and *Brick-Click* online sites such as Amazon, Walmart, Rakuten, Best Buy, Wayfair, Etsy, and eBay. *eCommerce* digitally connects Business-to-Business and Direct-to-Consumer. Banking has moved from Main Street to mainframe online with Discover, Axos, or Ally banking.

American workers who want to stay employed must keep pace with the digital and technology skills of redesigned future jobs. They must *embrace and take advantage of changes.* They must evaluate current job or career positions through shorter time frames of two years, one year, half a year, or less, depending upon age, opportunities for growth in the company's sector, or type of employment. Openness to change may be uncomfortable but can be improved by positive attitudes of learning and relearning. Anticipating tomorrow is demanding. But these challenges of openness, learning, and anticipating are easier than regret, frustration, and despair of looking backward. It is either forward or backward today. The easier path is being prepared for tomorrow.

CAIRN 10: MAKING EFFICIENT LIFE CHOICES

"The purpose of learning is growth, and our minds, unlike our bodies, can continue growing as we continue to live."

--Mortimer Adler

Economic citizens must continue to learn and learn how to learn. Understanding the new economic citizenship seems hard to come by. Americans may be ill-prepared in their schooling and fail to see their economic lives much beyond the job's weekly or bi-weekly paycheck and their bank balances. While important decisions are made on both the employment and consumer fronts, people find out too late that there was an informational asymmetry that favored firms. Asymmetrical information places consumers and prospective employees at a disadvantage. Care and vigilance must be given to gather important and relevant information. Information symmetry will improve consumers' and prospective employees' economic decisions.

Econ-Angst interferes with care and vigilance. It has the effects of freezing reasoning and clinging to emotion. Fast-moving economic encounters result in a type of economic sclerosis, hardening a person's place in and outlook of the economy. Economic citizenship requires the flexibility of constant schooling, training, skill development, product research, and vertical and horizon planning. It is not enough just to have a job. The new economic citizenship requires education and intelligence to be aware of the constantly morphing economy and the power forces that move it.

Historically, there have been whole job categories that disappeared in industries that were revolutionized or slowly diminished. Coal miners, switchboard operators, bowling alley pin setters (remember?), data entry workers, travel agents, warehouse workers, auto and factory line workers, secretaries of all types, and retail clerk positions are just a few. Economists call this a form of "creative destruction.[25]" It refers to freeing resources to construct a more efficient and productive economy by phasing out human resource skills and the physical capital of old techniques, machinery, and technology. Technological advancement and Artificial Intelligence will augur a new wave of job categories and professions in such areas as health practitioners, medical doctors, pharmacists, lawyers, writers, and educators. Short-sighted companies and industries will fall victim to change. The early 20th

Century railroad companies thought they were in the railroad industry until they realized they had missed their chance to dominate the transportation industry. The later 20th Century "car" was not on the tracks.

Career and job choices are opportunities for Econ-Angst reduction. The efficiency of labor and business decisions depends upon reading the economic tea leaves of economic growth and sector changes. Younger employees and business owners may make four *or more* changes in their working landscape over a lifetime. Steppingstone careers and businesses may be necessary to manage economic success and to aim at a later-in-life comfortable position.

Making efficient choices involves more than the employment side of the economy. The consumer side of the economy demands spending efficiency. Americans have grown and lived in the celebration of consumption for one hundred years. Twentieth Century industries mass-produced consumer goods that decreased consumer prices so lower classes could emulate upper-class luxuries. The mantra for most consumer goods from clothes to cars was more and bigger was better. Producers used *planned obsolescence* to prime the consumption pump. Producing products with reduced life sold more over time. It started in 1924 when the light-bulb cartel conspired to shorten the light bulb's lifespan. Companies in computers, smart phone technology, fashion, and autos have continued to force consumers to replace rather than repair and to persuade consumers to discard existing products for newer designs or models. Shelf life is the term given to home appliances and consumer entertainment products; Mr. Appliance (mrappliance.com) charts average life expectancies of most home appliances as little over a decade. The pace of consumer goods as "new and improved" has accelerated. For many reasons, older model electronic products are replaced because repair parts and services dry up. These factors contribute to the consumption strategy of the "throw-away" pattern of wasting economic and planet resources. This characteristic of the American economy of the last 70 years has hastened resource scarcity.

The modern consumer credit system was created to increase consumer demand when, in 1919, General Motors Acceptance Corporation first made installment payments available to qualified car buyers. The 1920s now had purchase contracts that were no longer cash at the point of sale. Installments on higher-priced purchases were instituted. They were followed by available bank credit, available store credit, and, in 1950, the revolving credit card led by the Diners Club. The Federal Housing Authority was established in 1934 to make home ownership mortgages cheaper and more available to certain neighborhoods of the country. By the middle of the century, "cash on the barrel" was replaced by "buy now, pay later."

The marketing and advertising industries have substituted product information with an emotional "feel good" experience of beautiful scenes, people, children, babies, and talking animals. Why not change colors for a new phone, car, or house interior? Color as an opinion has become a reason to purchase—it makes you feel better! Henry Ford said that the Model T could be bought in any color the customer wanted, as long as it was black, and, in 1919, that was the color that rolled out of the factory. Today, car manufacturers research in-fashion colors and finishes to increase sales of new models. It may be true that today a car can be found in any color.

While riding this wave of change, life occurs. Major economic decisions must continue to be made for marriage, partnering, children, job and profession changes, educational commitments, resident moving, and retirement. These life moments are usually of high Econ-Angst. Economic Cairns 10 focuses on making efficient work and consumer choices an integral part of the journey so that when these additional emotional burdens occur, you can still move forward.

CHAPTER 7

HIGHLIGHTS

THE NEW ECONOMIC CITIZENSHIP

- *The framework for easing Econ-Angst with the New Economic Citizenship.*
- *Building trust in the economy.*
- *Playing it smart with Economic Cairns*

"You miss 100% of the shots you don't take."

--Wayne Gretzky

"When the facts change, I change my mind. What do you do?"

--John Maynard Keynes

THE NEW ECONOMIC CITIZENSHIP

Economic citizenship in America has the advantage of economic freedom with its opportunities for success in an established legal environment. This citizenship is not awarded but earned. It is a journey of decisions with risks and rewards. Citizens start from and will land on a wide income and wealth spectrum. The United States Census Bureau measures inequalities by demographic factors. Historically, there is a general picture of inequalities in income[1] and wealth[2] between lower groups and the wealthy. About 12% of the 2022 US population live below the poverty line[3].

Much has been debated about the causes of income and wealth inequalities. Is it in the nature of American Capitalism? Is it caused by natural differences in abilities? Probably, but there are others. Viewing out the eco-self window, one sees equity differences in opportunities such as those of immigration status, gender, ethnicity, and race.

There are differences that are the result of social prejudice and institutional bias that have generational consequences.

The previous chapters presented a roadmap of valuable economic principles. The guide to new economic citizenship will *not* answer your questions about specific choices in investments, careers, employment, or educational opportunities. These are your responsibilities according to your situations and plans for success. The guide *is not a workbook but a framework.* The guide adds knowledge and principled concepts that put you in position to ease Econ-Angst. It is new because *economic citizenship has been revised for the demands of the 21st Century's economy*. Each Cairn explains an economic key to inform your *approach to economic life. Applying the Economic Cairns reduces Econ-Angst. This was our mission.* But by applying Cairns' economic concepts, you may make better decisions for economic success, however you define it.

Understanding the concepts will make it easier to confront future changes in the economy. The concepts will not change, but their applications will. Following Economic

Cairns will help you develop starting points, strategies, and goals. The journey to success will be more informed and reasoned.

A citizen must trust the economic system while understanding its pitfalls and inequalities. Trust is necessary to play by the rules and implement success strategies. Trust reduces Econ-Angst. The principle of Cairns is to navigate the headwinds of economic power and influences that blow income and wealth inequalities your way. Wandering off the path of the new economic citizenship by missing the markers of Economic Cairns will lead to emotional distress and false strategies of the "blame game," the "excuse game," the "gambling game," or the "underground illegal game."

The drive of the new economic citizenship is the power to overcome capitalism's shortcomings. Amassing asset wealth, idolizing individual freedom, and ignoring public goods needs to be left in the last century. As we move through the third decade of this century, we need the cultural change of the new economic citizenship.

Some values must be adjusted so that we can level income and asset wealth accumulation, highlight the common good, strive for social coherence, and take responsibility for our only home planet.

The drive for economic efficiency is the power to control existential scarcity. The new economic citizen has the power to change to the behaviors that lessen our Econ-Angst. Economic Cairns make the struggle easier. *There is no magic bullet solution. Playing smart is the move to make.*

Playing It Smart

USING SELF-KNOWLEDGE ECO-SELF PERSPECTIVES

You need to spend the effort to create a successful and efficient eco-self that will be valuable to you, to the economy, and to the planet.

This Cairn is primary. To be more emotionally comfortable, a citizen must adopt an economic stance that is aware of the horizontal and vertical place within the economy.

Horizontal means seeing work opportunities now and over time—the bigger box, and vertical means reaching higher socio-economic levels by seizing what life has to offer—the taller box.

Your sense of self has many facets. You have one sense of self for your friends and another for your family and relatives. You may act differently and feel differently with these groups. Your sense of self with family and friends probably came naturally through association and time. As a student, you had to create a learner-self while in a school or classroom. The eco-self was developed in the workplace and as a consumer. In these facets, your actions and feelings are created to appreciate and take advantage for your family, social group, educational, and economic roles.

Preparation and education are part of what is necessary to *see* yourself in various opportunities and levels of jobs and careers. You must be able to imagine yourself there. You must have that "serious talk" to awaken yourself to create your eco-self. Eco-self must assess and evaluate your abilities, characteristics, strengths, and weaknesses. It will create motivation and develop self-confidence and self-determination. It will discover opportunities. If you have a poorly developed eco-self, economic forces can take you anywhere. Any economic role will do.

After taking stock of your eco-self and the wide world of the economy, what do you visualize yourself doing? What knowledge do you need to overcome current difficulties and grasp future work possibilities? You need to believe in yourself to find easier success paths. At 60 years of age, you do not want to say, "I always wanted to be a ..."

Fighting the demands of success is hard enough. You do not want to also be fighting yourself. Use the mirror and the window.

ADDRESSING THE SCARCITY PROBLEM

Resource scarcity is **the** challenge of the 21st Century's economy; efficiency and proper resource allocation will reduce SET and Econ-Angst.

OK, you understand that your available resources, including your time and energy, are limited. You must operate from a position of scarcity on the road to success; make budgets and follow them. Wasting resources through inefficiency will increase your SET triggering an upward tension spiral. Being efficient in what and how you behave will make you feel as if you are "getting someplace." This will reduce SET and make further decision-making easier.

This Cairn is a practical study for using fewer resources for intended outcomes. Your eco-self will seek goals in the face of scarcity. Use less time, gas, electricity, entertainment costs, food wastage, and consumption expenditures. Spend less time on the phone and on social media. Make and fix planning strategies. Aim your energy at goals. Trade in some down time and screen time for productive time. Neil Postman's 1985 *Amusing Ourselves to Death* warned of the infusion of entertainment into daily life, including politics, journalism, education, and religion. This infusion has grown with the reliance on technologies that can erode the responsibilities of the new economic citizenship. We can longer afford the party behind the castle walls.

Scarcity and resource-wastage diminish your value to society and to yourself. *You can be worth more than you think!*

PROMOTING ECONOMIC COMPETITION+

The new view of competition will change the idea of winning in the economy.

Economic competition+ is a stretch, especially for those who have had an economic course. You must realize that you are an important part of the economy. You are competing for your economic, social, and environmental value. All three are equally important. Actualizing yourself in the competitive+ world, resists the sports-type of competition of trying to win the game's trophy or the goal of greed. Greed and winning the material race is seductive. You are in wage and consumer competition with workers around the globe. You are in competition to advance cooperative improvements needed for community cohesion, including youth coaching and activities, group projects, food banks, teaching evening adult education, volunteering for fire and emergency services, and organizing medical equipment swaps. Economic competition+ expands advantages in all communities, cities, and nations. Winning this competition+ is measured by winning with friends and community, winning for social cohesion, and winning for the planet's health.

Economic competition+ places corporate planning for environmental actions on par with profitable actions. It places government environmental actions on par with other budget items. Echoes of the 1970s ecological warnings resound in today's board rooms and Congressional committees. Business labor relations are a complex mix of matching needs to skills, maintaining productive relationships with subcontracted entities, managing remote workers' productivity, and coordinating global communications of the company. Corporate management must juggle government regulations, supply chain issues, global competition, and *climate change*. Businesses must be good neighbors and community members, not polluters of air and water and not contributors to traffic and transportation problems. Caring for employees may include activities outside the office or warehouse walls. Assessment of environmental damage is imperative. Now is the time to recycle, renew, redesign, renovate, and plan to heal the planet. A great effort is needed at the individual, local, and national levels. Remember the slogan, "Think globally, act locally!" The new economic citizenship demands economic competition+.

The choice of career is an important part of economic competition+. It is a dedication to advantages that go beyond a paycheck. Choosing or changing to helping careers such as environmental research, medicine, education, law, policing, security, safety, and medical arts are pro-social and pro-planet. Economists see these careers as creators of positive external benefits to society and the earth. The value of saving, educating, or improving a life goes beyond the point of service. Other careers such as biochemistry, social planning, agricultural research, architecture, technology, and automation applications have a role to play in planet sustainability.

Citizens must be able to promote the three tiers of competition+. Economic competition+ operates at three levels, (1) economic (business and consumer) competition, (2) competition for society's improvement, and (3) competition for a livable planet. *Econ-Angst can dissolve into satisfaction with winning in the economic competition+.*

RECOGNIZING OPPORTUNITY COSTS

Calculating Opportunity Costs proves that nothing is free. Do not practice naive economics. A careful approach that considers opportunity benefits and costs reduces Econ-Angst.

Gathering all the benefits and costs of making important economic decisions is comforting. Testing the decision over longer time spans brings the current into better focus. More knowledge can control panic and nervousness. Realizing the costs of opportunity lost is vital in a resource-scarce world. The amount of time, human energy, non-renewable energy, and physical resources are limited. Doing the other thing is the opportunity cost of doing the one thing. The time learning economics might cost the time watching a feature motion picture. Working overtime might cost family time. Buying a new refrigerator might cost repairs on the second car. Resources used in building a bridge might cost a new wing of the overcrowded middle school. Recognizing the opportunity costs brings efficiency to decision-making.

Making decisions without knowing the opportunity costs is *naïve economics.* It is naïve because decisions are made as if by children who don't understand the true cost of the alternative. Time and resources cannot be replaced once spent. Even if you did not pay for your lunch sandwich, it is not free. The bread, turkey, and provolone were resource costs. Someone had to raise the turkey, bake the bread, and produce the provolone. Someone had to transport them to the restaurant, and someone had to make the sandwich. None of these economic activities were free; they all had alternative activity opportunity costs. Granted, you did not pay for the sandwich, but it was not free to the economy. *Opportunity lost is opportunity cost. Time lost is a severe cost.*

USING MARGINAL ANALYSIS

Making decisions at each step (at the margin) increases accuracy and efficiency.

Most complex activities involve processes that can be divided into steps. Analysis is looking at the steps or pieces of a problem. Construction contractors use flow charts. Cooks use step-by-step recipes. Dancers break down a performance into steps (literally). Mathematical algorithms are carefully developed calculative steps. Economists make decisions and solve problems not in total but at the margins, the next step or part.

The new economic citizen must follow the same process. Jumping to solutions and decisions hides the devil in the details. It does not give you room to consider alternatives and parallel thoughts. You need to keep your eye on the overall goal or conclusion and, at the same time, see steps as thought-pauses toward an end. Difficult and important decisions arc usually complex, with smaller choices buried inside. Process decisions must be made at the margin, the next step. Does the enjoyment value of entertainment's last hour match its additional cost? Is the sale price of the last production run worth the cost of that item? Is the all-inclusive cost at the resort worth all the things I have done? Break down the a la carte charges to see. *Slow down decision-making for each step.*

LIVING BY A NEW WORK ETHIC

Realize there is no easy way in the evolving nature of work.

Younger workers' view of work.

The post-industrial work has evolved from its agricultural (sunup to sundown) and industrial (8-hour shifts) beginnings. It is time for a new concept of work to conform to modern life. Advances in economic uses of technology, automation, robotics, digital applications, and Artificial

Intelligence are changing the work landscape. Generations Z (birth between 1997-2012) and A (between 2012-?) will need a post-industrial education and aptitude for stretching the learning years well into the future. The younger workers are facing new opportunities and demands for labor.

They are not preparing for *the job or a job;* they realize that a job or career is not a lifetime investment. They are part of the employment carousel. And, if it is not what they want to do with their lives, then why play for keeps. It is rational. The loyalty bond between employer and employee is broken because neither party can serve up the long term. During the Great Resignation of 2021, employees left their jobs in record numbers. Low pay, lack of advancement, lack of flexibility, and lack of respect were among the reasons.

Younger workers do not see work being the only thing in life. They build generalized technology skills and analytic attitudes that will fit many jobs or can be expanded into future jobs. They do not see any ladder for success. They yearn for expectations of the virtual world. They have gotten used to the thrill of instant gratification. They want to travel, live in different states or countries, study or work abroad, or visit social media friends face-to-face. Their neighborhood is much bigger than the school district's neighborhood and phone number exchange of last century.

Older workers' view of work.

When checking older workers (many who have had to re-skill on the fly), we see another attitude about the younger generation. Older workers have been "schooled" in an industrial classroom schedule or may remember the industrial work world. The vanishing industrial world of work said:

- *get the job,*
- *punch the clock,*
- *follow the bells and schedules,*
- *just work your station,*
- *do your job; you don't get paid to think,*

- *work at least five days a week, fifty weeks a year,*
- *retire around 62 years of age, and*
- *live on savings, pension(?), and Social Security.*

There was a physicality to many of last century's jobs. Older workers tend to see jobs as fixed positions in the employment egg crate of the economy. They see the younger ones as soft or pampered. They see them as looking for down time, vacations, or long weekends. They don't see them as having the patience to climb the ladder of success.

We have moved or are moving past this work environment, but the *perception* that older workers and professionals have is younger workers do not want to work. They don't want to work hard or put in the necessary hours and days. They do not have the grit and motivation anymore. They are not working as hard as we did to get ahead.

Healing the communication failure.

Younger workers have one view of the work world, and older workers have another. This is caused by rapid structural changes in the economy with neither group talking about the same idea of work and job. This confusion can be improved by fleshing out the differences.

From today's viewpoint, Twentieth Century workplace conditions were in place for a longer time span and changes occurred at a slower pace. Those entering the workforce looked to land one chosen job. Children tended to enter their parents' (usually the father's) line of work. Jobs and careers ran in the family: my parents worked at the factory, so I'll work at the factory; father worked in the mine, so I'll work in the mine; mother was a teacher, so I'll be a teacher; father was a fire fighter, so I'll be a fire fighter.

For Generation Z and Generation A, the parents may not have had a lifelong job, but if they did, they might be telling the kids not to apply for it. Twentieth Century jobs may still be extant but may be extinct or diminishing.

How can the two perceptions of work be combined? The Twenty-first Century's concept of hard work needs renewal. The older attitudes of working hard must change to include skills of technology and not physicality. The new century introduces a wider expanse of opportunities such as the creative arts, journalism, writing, performing, new and innovative technology development, environment and ecology sciences, green transformation businesses, economics, and government services. Careers and jobs in these areas demand higher education and tech-skill levels that do not show up as old-school, physically hard, or static enough. *They are hard in another way; from the digital world, they are brain and thinking hard; from the employment world, they are more transitory.*

The workplaces are changing or have changed. There may not be one workstation with a standard time on task. Workers on the floor and in offices will work in team environments with enormous access to data and software programs. There may be a casualness and flexibility about breaks, lunch, and workstation configurations. Hybrid office work models differ from the 9 to 5 work-in-place with a break room. It is a mixture of virtual and face-to-face communication, in-office, out-of-office, and remote time.

The increase in service industries has added flexibility and uniqueness to employee-consumer connections.

It may be difficult to make sense of this century's work world. But Robert Reich in *The Work of Nations: Preparing Ourselves for the 21st Century* (1991) carved out three emerging work categories. Each category had different work expectations and skills. They were: (1) *routine production services* where employees were valued for reliability, loyalty, and ability to take direction; (2) *in-person services* where employees had the same three qualities plus a pleasing demeanor; and (3) *symbolic-analytic services* where employees were required to have problem-solving, problem-identifying, and strategic-brokering skills for symbolic language and mathematical manipulations. The first category was in decline, while the last two showed increasing percentages in the workforce.

For the new work ethic, businesses must reconsider employee well-being and productivity in the workplace culture. New measures of productivity are needed for team output and creative output. Work breaks must be redesigned to take into consideration the digitalized and thought-intense worktime.

Twenty-first Century employees, however, still must have an older work ethic of responsibility, trust, honesty, finishing what was started, meeting deadlines, and pride in quality. The 20th Century employees must adapt their approach to the work ethic by seeing that technology skills transfer beyond the job. They must loosen the walls that define their employment and enjoy change as a survival skill. *The new work ethic must match the needs of the employees, the employer, and the economy.*

INVESTING IN YOURSELF

Calculate the payout of formal and informal education.

You want to make yourself as valuable as possible to the economy and an asset to the employer. Learning to improve marketable knowledge and skills is a rewarding activity. *Economists see workers as human capital; businesses see you as a productive input; you must see yourself as a flexible income investment.* Employers hire your worth as measured by time-on-task or output-per-time-unit. They do not hire you for *what you are worth.* They only see you as the value of a production input, in other words, the productivity of your time. Your eco-self must see your worth differently. It must be seen as the bundle of skills, knowledge, and attitudes that are fungible in the labor market. You exist as a marketable investment. In this way, an employer will never pay you what you are worth. If a science public school teacher takes a summer job behind a counter, the store pays her only what she is worth for her time on job. The store will not pay her what she is actually worth to the economy.

Eco-self is the power source that produces value in three ways: (1) by satisfactory personal income, (2) by efficient economic productivity to society, and (3) by having the least resource footprint on the earth. These three ways must be goals of the new economic citizenship. Economists see public, private, and informal education as investments in the economy. You must see education as an investment in yourself.

The path to economic success demands keeping a current knowledge base and skill set along the way. This eases the Econ-Angst of the twists and turns of the 21st Century workspace. The new economic citizen takes self-investment seriously. Investment installments paid to yourself will have a better dollar return over your work-age span than other investment opportunities. Invest in yourself the same way you would invest in any other asset by placing money from a paycheck periodically toward formal education or informal learning experiences.

Income from you-as-investment is calculated in dollars and in "psychic income." Employees and business owners who work *just* for the money will not be as satisfied as those who also earn psychic income. Psychic income comes from the satisfaction and happiness of an economic activity that works for you and for the betterment of others and the environment. It is an opportunity benefit. You can tailor investment in upgraded knowledge and skills to provide positive returns of making others better off and contributing to the planet's health. Without some element of psychic income, the only way to compensate for the loss of satisfaction is to work harder for more hours per year and more years per lifetime. More dollars for happiness? Maybe.

There are ways to invest in yourself. You must find the right balance of the three ways to make yourself valuable. Your investment payout is a measure of success. *You are your most controllable asset.*

BRANDING YOURSELF

You must begin constructing "You as the product." How do you brand yourself?

Last century's industrialized economy viewed employees as generic and replaceable workers. It usually did not matter if the employee was young or middle-aged, tall, short, blonde, or bald, as long as the basic job requirements were met. However, the new economic citizenship must address changes in employment workplaces and new eco-work attitudes and social skills.

Branding yourself is a competitive advantage. You know that matching skills with job and career requirements benefits hiring and promotions. This is the first step in branding yourself. Gaining specific knowledge and skills increases employment chances. New skills are needed. They include the skills of learning acumen, collaboration, creativity, information literacy, technology, communication, writing, critical thinking, analyzing, synthesizing, problem-solving, leadership, emotional intelligence, flexibility, self-management, and self-motivation. However, a standout personality of compatibility, humor, dependability, diversity appreciation, or unselfishness, can be the second step of your branding. Authentic work personalities are appreciated and, at times, celebrated. The recognition that you earn with your eco-self, specific knowledge, and skills will elevate your brand in the workplace or team. *Bring more than your body to work; bring a valuable brand of yourself!*

REALIZING THE ONLY CONSTANT IS CHANGE

Know the pace of change because tomorrow is this morning.

The pace of change has increased this century for technology tools, communications, entertainment sourcing, consumption purchasing, news availability, and short-term information processing. Econ-Angst increases with the feeling of being "left behind" or even "left out." The generational time frame for life becomes Life 2.0 or Life 3.0 and beyond. It begs questions.

- *What should I remember?*
- *What should I forget?*
- *What should I learn?*
- *Where should I place work environments . . . in short-term or long-term memory?*

The answer to these questions revolves around the importance of your goals and aims. You need to *be selective* in receiving and processing the myriad media messages. Focusing on *your path* is a needed skill.

The 1961 Broadway Musical, *Stop the World, I Want to Get Off*, may have new relevance six decades later for the new economic citizen. Seeing the economy as snap shots is not the way forward. It is better to experience it as a documentary film or a long novel where you cannot wait to see what happens next. Embrace dynamism, not stasis. The anticipation skill must be honed so that seeing what is going to happen next is just as real as what is happening now. Anticipation in sports makes a player more successful. Anticipating economic life will make a citizen more successful. Seeing further down the road improves a driver's ability not to be surprised. Seeing further down the economic road improves the business and employment ability to ease Econ-Angst. *Be the director of your own economic movie.*

MAKING EFFICIENT LIFE CHOICES

There is learning by doing.

Follow the ten Cairns for an easier economic journey.

1. *Know who you are in the new economy.*

2. *Know where you are in the new economy.*
3. *Know how to compete in the new economy.*
4. *Know all costs before making decisions.*
5. *Plan and improve step-by-step.*
6. *Know how, and how hard it is to work in the new economy.*
7. *Invest wisely in yourself for the new economy.*
8. *Advertise who you are and what you are worth.*
9. *Go fast enough to stay current.*
10. *Do not waste the opportunities you have.*

We now know that efficiency has three layers—the personal, society's economic, and the environmental. Our eco-self must organize these three. It is your decision to become a new economic citizen, and, after reading this far, you are better prepared. Econ-Angst derives from not knowing what is ahead on the economic path to success. Powerful economic points encased in the Cairns will give you more knowledge from out your window and a sense of empowerment from your image in the mirror. The first Cairn is the starting point for your new economic internship. The other nine are arranged in an order that makes sense to me. Choosing where to begin the other nine will depend upon your eco-self and experiences.

Knowing and doing are two of life's separate skill compartments. How many times have we done something that we know we should not have? How many times have we done something without knowing if it was the right thing? How many times have we done something just for the fun of it? Yeah.

We must combine knowing and doing in economic life. Living a purposeful life defines intentions. Decreasing Econ-Angst while improving your place in the economy is an ideal way of *constructing success*. Following Economic Cairns will do this. But thoughts and intentions alone are not enough. Actions and results measure the journey. As the former football Giants coach, Bill Parcells, once said about his underperforming team: *"It's not how good you think you are; it's what your record says you are."*

As an educator working with students, many group discussions were held to define success. They were lively and informative. More questions were raised than answered.

- *My father spent most of his time working. Was that being successful?*
- *My mother and father had full-time jobs. Were we successful?*
- *Is having four cars being successful?*
- *Is my family successful if I only see cousins on holidays?*
- *Is working on weekends the best way to succeed?*
- *Can you get sick by being successful?*
- *Are air quality and temperature warnings part of our success?*
- *Is the long line at the food bank part of our success?*

The definition of success must be defined individually. Seeing economic success through the *prism of the new economic citizenship* encompasses seeing a wider view of the workspace, being socially responsible, and caring for the earth's sustainability. This applies to any of the roles played in the economy, whether owner, manager, or employee. It will bring more satisfaction and comfort while striving.

Your personal view of economic success is not the only one, but it is the most important one for America's success. Citizens knowing and meeting the responsibilities of the new economic citizen can realize a more equitable standard of living, greater social cohesion, and proper stewardship of the earth. That is the way a democratic economy works, one at a time. In a democracy, new economic citizenship is *the* step in the right direction. Each of us is a necessary piece of the country's economic puzzle.

APPENDIX

Sites for New Economic Citizens

1. Census Bureau Index of Economic Activity (IDEA)

The IDEA is an indexed combination of fifteen of the Bureau's data series that tracks the country's economic activity. The trend lines show periods of growth, retraction, and recession.

https://www.census.gov/econ_assets/econindex/index.html#:~:text=Notes%3A-,The%20U.S.%20Census%20Bureau%20Index%20of%20Economic%20Activity%20(IDEA)%20is,and%20estimated%20monthly%20growth%20rates

2. Consumer Confidence Index (CCI)

The Conference Board (a non-profit think tank based in New York) uses the CCI to measure consumer attitudes about their financial prospects.

https://www.investopedia.com/terms/c/conference-board.asp

3. Economic Indicators

There are many economic indicators used by private and government groups to measure the economy's direction. The most common are the Consumer Price Index, the Gross Domestic Product, as well as the unemployment rate, consumption, investment, the international trade balance, and government budgets. They are divided into leading, coincident, and lagging indicators.

https://www.investopedia.com/terms/e/economic_indicator.asp#:~:text=Economic%20indicators%20such%20as%20GDP,policy%20or%20set%20investment%20strategies.

4. Misery Index

The misery index is a 1970s concept describing a country's economic unease. It is calculated by combining the two economic data points of inflation and unemployment rate. The index number is a useful indicator of *overall economic health*. The higher the misery index, the greater the country's misery.

MI = UNEMPLOYMENT RATE + INFLATION RATE

A "normal" U.S. rate for the Misery Index is considered to be between 5.5 and 6.5. The higher the rate, the more misery in the economy.

For example, if the unemployment rate (seasonally adjusted) is 4% and the inflation rate (Consumer Price Index) is 3%, then the Misery Index would be 7, which is considered higher than normal.

https://www.investopedia.com/terms/m/miseryindex.asp#:~:text=The%20misery%20index%20is%20calculated,indicator%20of%20overall%20economic%20health.

5. Reports of Economic Well-Being

General well-being is difficult to measure because it is largely subjective. Even though, The Centers for Disease Control and Prevention have attempted to define and measure well-being. It is a loosely constructed concept but is important because of its relationship to Econ-Angst. Economic well-being and life satisfaction show up as primary factors. In the five surveys used by the CDC, dependence for life satisfaction was more closely tied "to availability of basic needs being met (food, shelter, income) as well as access to modern conveniences (e.g., electricity)."

https://www.cdc.gov/hrqol/wellbeing.htm#five

6. World Happiness Report

This report is published by Sustainable Development Solutions Network and the Gallup World Poll data. It surveys countries' attitudes in six areas: GDP per person, social support, healthy life expectancy, freedom, generosity, and corruption. Countries are ranked according to their citizens' responses. The United States ranked 16th in the 2023 report.

https://wisevoter.com/country-rankings/happiest-countries-in-the-world/

7. United States Economic and Demographic Profiles

Economic and demographic information is available at the US Census Bureau. There are several tables showing employment, education, and income profiles, with many available by age, sex, or race/ethnicity.

https://www.census.gov/acs/www/data/data-tables-and-tools/subject-tables/

8. Public Misconceptions

1. **Demand is a quantity**. *No. It is the relationship between prices and quantities demanded.*
2. **Supply is a quantity**. *No. It is the relationship between prices and quantities supplied.*
3. **The stock market is a good measure of the economy.** *No. Stock markets are derivative of more basic measures of the economy such as unemployment and inflation. Standard and Poor's 500 Index is an imperfect leading indicator and is one of ten typically used. The stock market is not the economy, but rather a consensus of investor confidence and attitude.*

4. **Everyone has a good chance to become wealthy.** *Hardly. The odds of becoming wealthy (a billionaire?) are very slim (in the single digits) and become slimmer when age and race are considered. Most become rich through inheritance.*

5. **Wealth is money.** *No. Money is primarily a medium of exchange. It is a poor symbolic store of value but is not economic wealth. Wealth is amassed through asset and production ownership.*

6. **Money is backed by gold.** *No. Not since 1971 when President Nixon took gold from backing the dollar. The current US dollar is considered fiat money backed only by the public's general acceptance and by the full faith and credit of the U.S. government and taxpayers.*

7. **Gold is wealth.** *No. Like money gold is a symbolic store of value. It has an advantage of protecting value in inflationary times. King Midas learned his lesson.*

8. **America is the healthiest country in the world.** *Far from it. America ranks well below the top twenty-five in most measurements of life expectancy, chronic diseases, obesity, and infant mortality. Its health system lags most advanced countries.*

9. **America is the freest country in the world.** *No. The United States just makes it into the top fifteen rankings. Switzerland, New Zealand, and Denmark are the top three, according to World Population Review.*

10. **Americans, on average, are the richest citizens in the world.** *No. Countries such as Luxembourg, Bermuda, Ireland, Norway, Qatar, and Switzerland have higher average incomes.*

11. **Technological innovation is the answer to environmental degradation.** *The jury is out on this one. It does not seem to be* ***the answer,*** *but it may be one of many parts. Technology has proved to be a saving factor for many climate and ecological dangers.*

However, there is evidence that its assistance to the world's productivity has done environmental harm.

12. **More is better than less**. *Not really. This consumer mantra has been criticized by economists, environmental scientists, ecology organizations, and climatologists. The 1973 book, Small Is Beautiful, by E. F. Schumacher made the case that capitalism's growth would need to place the needs of people and the environment above excessive economic growth. Half a century later, it seems that the challenge of "more is better" has threatened resources and humanity's quality of life. Doing more with less has emerged as the new calling for the finite resources of Spaceship Earth.*

EXPLANATORY ECONOMIC TERMS

Econ-Angst -- *the pervasive and general feeling of unease and anxiety caused by economic stressors.*

Economic competition+ -- *the extension of market demand-and- supply competition to include the economy's competition for social well-being and the competition to maintain and save earth's sustainability.*

Economic sclerosis – *a term originating with the economist, Mancor Olson, in The Rise and Decline of Nations (1984), that refers to rigidity of mature companies. It is used here to refer to the rigidity of workers' employment movement.*

Eco-self – *short for your economic self-concept that operates in a work, business, or consumer atmosphere that promotes the confidence to progress and succeed.*

Fantasy economics – *a strategy for success based on emotion and chance payoffs including betting, gaming, and make-believes.*

Naïve economics – *the economic approach to decision making that does not include opportunity costs* (not to be confused with similar terms that have been used variously in economic theory and Behavioral Economics).

Scarcity-Efficiency Tension (SET) – *the emotional response that occurs when there is a gap between scarcity level and efficiency level within economic activities.*

END NOTES

INTRODUCTION

[1] The United Nations International Labor Organization. (2023). Americans annually work more hours than six developed countries used in the study: More than Australia, the United Kingdom, Sweden, Belgium, France, and Germany.

[2] Zippia, The Career Expert. (2023). Average work hours per week. Retrieved from

https://www.zippia.com/advice/average-work-hours-per-week/#:~:text=The%20average%20American%20adult%20works%2038.7%20hours%20per%20week.&text=That%20works%20out%20to%20spending,most%20of%20any%20age%20group

[3] Money. (2023). Americans work longer hours compared to Europe and China.

Retrieved from: https://money.com/americans-work-hours-vs-europe-china/

CHAPTER ONE

[1]. Council for Economic Education. (2022). Survey of the states. Retrieved from

https://www.councilforeconed.org/policy-advocacy/survey-of-the-states/

[2] Good Society Forum. (2020). Using K-12 schools to promote civic engagement. *Good Society, 29*(1-2), 74. Retrieved from

https://scholarlypublishingcollective.org/psup/good-society/article-abstract/29/1-2/74/319568/Using-K-12-Schools-to-Promote-Civic-Engagement?redirectedFrom=fulltext

[3] Brown University. (2022). Economic stress. Retrieved from

https://www.brown.edu/campus-life/health/services/promotion/general-health-emotional-

health/economic-stress#:~:text=experi-
ences%20of%20a%20job%20loss,to%20work%20while%20in%20college

[4] Brown University. (2022). Economic stress. Retrieved from

https://www.brown.edu/campus-life/health/services/promotion/general-health-emotional-health/economic-stress#:~:text=experiences%20of%20a%20job%20loss,to%20work%20while%20in%20college

[5] WebMD. (2021). What is scarcity mentality? Retrieved from

https://www.webmd.com/mental-health/what-is-scarcity-mentality

[6] NBC News. (June 27, 2022). Economic anxiety is replacing COVID fears. Retrieved from

https://www.nbcnews.com/think/opinion/economic-anxiety-replacing-COVID-fears-recession-stock-market-coping-rcna34892

[7] Verywell Mind. (August 7, 2022). What is the Econ Angst index? Retrieved from

https://www.verywellmind.com/what-is-the-Econ-Angst-index-5324863#:~:text=Anxiety%20levels%20tend%20to%20increase,more%20likely%20to%20save%20it

[8] American Psychological Association. (2017). State of Our Nation, November 2017.

[9] American Psychological Association. (2019). Gen Z stress report. Retrieved from

https://www.apa.org/monitor/2019/01/gen-z

[10] Marketplace. (2020). Economic Anxiety Index. Retrieved from

https://www.marketplace.org/2020/05/05/COVID-19-Econ-Angst-spike-food-groceries-rent-mortgages-health-care/

[11] American Psychological Association. (2022). Concerned about future inflation. Retrieved from

https://www.apa.org/news/press/releases/stress/2022/concerned-future-inflation

[12] Handshake. (January 15, 2018). New grad future of work. Retrieved from

https://joinhandshake.com/network-trends/new-grad-future-of-work/

[13] Healthline. (May 2023). Stress health costs. Retrieved from

https://www.healthline.com/health-news/stress-health-costs#:~:text=As%20a%20result%2C%20the%20authors,States%20%24300%20billion%20every%20year.

[14] Investopedia. (2022). Consumerism definition. Retrieved from

https://www.investopedia.com/terms/c/consumerism.asp

[15] Citi GPS: Global Perspectives & Solutions. (2022). Closing the racial inequality gaps: The economic cost of Black inequality in the U.S., September 2022.

[16] World Economic Forum. (2021). Racial and ethnic inequality has cost U.S. economy $51 trillion since 1990. Retrieved from

https://www.weforum.org/agenda/2021/09/racial-and-ethnic-inequality-has-cost-us-economy-51-trillion-since-1990/

[17] Statista. (July 24, 2023). Radio industry in the U.S. Retrieved from

https://www.statista.com/topics/1330/radio/

[18] Point Clicker. (January 26, 2023). How many TV channels are there in the USA? Retrieved from

https://pointerclicker.com/how-many-tv-channels-are-there-in-usa/#:~:text=So%2C%20if%20you%20want%20to,net-works%20in%20the%20United%20States.

[19] Statista. (May 16, 2023). Advertising in the U.S. Retrieved from

https://www.statista.com/topics/979/advertising-in-the-us/#topicOverview

[20] Verywell Health. (April 25, 2022). Phone addiction. Retrieved from

https://www.verywellhealth.com/phone-addiction-5218743

[21] Flurry. (March 2, 2017). US consumers' time spent on mobile crosses 5 hours per day. Retrieved from

https://www.flurry.com/blog/us-consumers-time-spent-on-mobile-crosses-5/

CHAPTER TWO

[1] Smith, A. (1776). An Inquiry into the Nature and Causes of The Wealth of Nations. Adam Smith associated a moral purpose with national wealth and the material well-being of its citizenry. He argued against Mercantilism and central government (royal) rule. A nation's wealth was not in the country's amount of gold and silver amassed, but rather, in its people's productive capacity--their education, freedom, self-interest, and motivation for improvement—leading to increased specialization and

economic invention and monitored by economic competition.

[2] The Business Insider. (June 26, 2014). Table: Different schools of economics. Retrieved from

https://www.businessinsider.com/table-different-schools-of-economics-2014-6?IR=T

Prominent economists include Ludwig von Mises, Friedrich Hayek, Joseph Schumpeter, Karl Marx, John Baptiste Say, John Maynard Keynes, Milton Friedman, John Kenneth Galbraith, Kenneth Boulding, Paul Samuelson, Paul Krugman, Amartya Sen, and others.

[3] Wikipedia. (October 31, 2018). Nobel Memorial Prizes in Economics. Retrieved from

https://en.wikiquote.org/wiki/Nobel_Memorial_Prize_in_Economic_Sciences

CHAPTER THREE

[1] A thought line can be traced from European thinkers such as Hobbes, Montesquieu, Smith, and Locke to Franklin, Jefferson, John Adams, and Madison.

CHAPTER SIX

[1] "Learning IQ" used here as a combination of five mental characteristics:

1. Openness to learning and relearning,
2. Curiosity,
3. Motivation,
4. Emotional Intelligence,
5. Understanding of Learning Styles.

[2] The organizations include Embracing Future Potential, Institute for the Future, Toffler Associates, MBO Partners, International Data Corporation, Gartner, World Economic Forum, Pearson, LinkedIn, and PwC.

[3] Career Addict. (2023). Disappearing jobs. Retrieved from

https://www.careeraddict.com/disappearing-jobs

[4] World Economic Forum. (2023). Global risks report. Retrieved from

https://www.weforum.org/reports/global-risks-report-2023/digest?_gl=1*1hus1ip*_up*MQ..&gclid=EAIaI-QobChMItLz1tMjU_gIVJQtlCh1k3QTZEAAYAi-AAEgIqTvD_BwE

[5] Kelton, S. (2020). The Deficit Myth: Modern Monetary Theory and the Birth of the People's Economy. Public Affairs.

[6] Gordon Gekko's character in the movie Wall Street (1987).

[7] Earth Day began in 1970 to bring attention to the harmful effects of human activity on the environment. Rachel Carson's Silent Spring (1962) rang the first warning bell of pesticide usage.

[8] FinanceBuzz. (August 15, 2023). U.S. net worth statistics: the state of wealth in 2023. Retrieved from

https://financebuzz.com/us-net-worth-statistics#:~:text=The%20top%20ten%20percent%20of,just%201%25%20of%20all%20wealth

[9] Linkedin. (2023). Skills First Report. Retrieved from

https://economicgraph.linkedin.com/content/dam/me/economicgraph/en-us/PDF/skills-first-report-2023.pdf

[10] Federal Reserve Economic Data. (2018). Corporate profits versus labor income. Retrieved from

https://fredblog.stlouisfed.org/2018/08/corporate-profits-versus-labor-income/

[11] Congressional Budget Office. (October 2, 2020). Trends in labor force participation. Retrieved from

https://www.cbo.gov/publication/55413

[12] Statista. (July 17, 2023). Wealth distribution for the U.S. Retrieved from

https://www.statista.com/statistics/203961/wealth-distribution-for-the-us/

[13] Cullen, J. (2003). The American Dream: A Short History of an Idea That Shaped a Nation. Oxford University Press.

[14] Weber, M., & Parsons, T. (1905). The Protestant Ethic and the Spirit of Capitalism: The Complete Text - Inclusive of Notes. Pantianos Classics.

[15] Anderson, K. (2018). Fantasyland. Random House.

[16] Federal Reserve Economic Data. (March 2023). Real disposable personal income per capita. Retrieved from

https://fred.stlouisfed.org/series/DGAMRC1A027NBEA

[17] Legal Sports Betting Review. (April 17, 2023). U.S. sports betting revenue & handle. Retrieved from

https://www.legalsportsreport.com/sports-betting/revenue/#:~:text=US%20Sports%20Betting%20Revenue%20%26%20Handle&text=The%20US%20sports%20betting%20industry,%24250%20billion%20in%20total%20wagers.

[18] U.S. Bureau of Labor Statistics. (2016). Union membership in the United States. Retrieved from

https://www.bls.gov/spotlight/2016/union-membership-in-the-united-states/home.htm#:~:text=The%20number%20of%20employed%20union,to%2011.1%20percent%20in%202015.

[19] Social Security Administration. (November 2015). Education and earnings. Retrieved from

https://www.ssa.gov/policy/docs/research-summaries/education-earnings.html#:~:text=Men%20with%20bachelor's%20degrees%20earn,earnings%20than%20high%20school%20graduates

[20] U.S. Bureau of Labor Statistics. (September 8, 2022). Unemployment rate and earnings by education. Retrieved from

https://www.bls.gov/emp/chart-unemployment-earnings-education.htm

[21] Social Security Administration. (September 8, 2022). Education and earnings. Retrieved from

https://www.ssa.gov/policy/docs/research-summaries/education-earnings.html#:~:text=Men%20with%20bachelor's%20degrees%20earn,earnings%20than%20high%20school%20graduates.

[22] National Center for Education Statistics. (2023). College enrollment rate. Retrieved from

https://nces.ed.gov/programs/coe/indicator/cpb/college-enrollment-rate

[23] Research. (July 27, 2023). Percentage of high school graduates that go to college. Retrieved from

https://research.com/education/percentage-of-high-school-graduates-that-go-to-college

[24] Forbes. (July 17, 2022). Why the digital nomad lifestyle is on the rise. Retrieved from

https://www.forbes.com/sites/carolinecastrillon/2022/07/17/why-the-digital-nomad-lifestyle-is-on-the-rise/?sh=3dc450854934

[25] Schumpeter, J. A. (1905). The Theory of Economic Development. Transaction Publishers.

CHAPTER SEVEN

[1] Investopedia. (May 20, 2022). A brief history of income inequality in the United States. Retrieved from

https://www.investopedia.com/articles/investing/110215/brief-history-income-inequality-united-states.asp

[2] Pew Research Center. (2020). Trends in income and wealth inequality. Retrieved from

https://www.pewresearch.org/social-trends/2020/01/09/trends-in-income-and-wealth-inequality/

[3] U.S. Census Bureau. (2022). Income and poverty in the United States: 2020. Retrieved from

https://www.census.gov/library/publications/2022/demo/p60-277.html

ABOUT THE AUTHOR

After completing an M.A. degree in economics at Columbia University, Dr. Erbe earned an M.S and Ed.D. in education. His vast teaching experience brought him success with students from the high school, undergraduate, and graduate levels as well as doctoral candidates. As a busy and resolute educator, he has consulted for the New Jersey Department of Education, worked with school districts to improve educational outcomes, and presented educational improvement programs nationally and internationally. In his diverse teaching career, he has worked with minority high school students, first- and second-generation immigrant college students, and at a women's university. He currently is an economics professor at a Florida college where he continues his successful learner friendly and learning friendly teaching style.

Made in the USA
Monee, IL
04 November 2026

67374644R00144